MW01196643

Releasing
Resurrection
and Revival

FROM THE

COURTS OF HEAVEN

Releasing Resurrection *and* Revival

FROM THE
COURTS OF HEAVEN

Prayers and
Declarations that
Raise Dead Things
to Life

ROBERT HENDERSON

DESTINY IMAGE® PUBLISHERS, INC.
P.O. Box 310, Shippensburg, PA 17257-0310
"Promoting Inspired Lives."

This book and all other Destiny Image and Destiny Image Fiction books are available at Christian bookstores and distributors worldwide.

For more information on foreign distributors, call 717-532-3040.

Reach us on the Internet: www.destinyimage.com.

ISBN 13 HC: 978-0-7684-6008-7

ISBN 13 eBook: 978-0-7684-6009-4

ISBN 13 TP: 978-0-7684-6010-0

For Worldwide Distribution, Printed in the U.S.A.

1 2 3 4 5 6 7 8 / 26 25 24 23 22

CONTENTS

CHAPTER 1

THE SPIRIT OF RESURRECTION

Most leaders and people I know believe that if we haven't already entered a place of awakening and revival, we are headed there. I vehemently agree with this assessment. With all the challenges we are presently facing on a worldwide platform, it would seem that people's hearts would now be open for God to manifest Himself in unprecedented ways. This is what I believe we are going to see. Just like the occurrence in Mark 2:12 when the four men tore a hole in the roof to get their friend into Jesus' presence, he rose and walked from his paralytic state. The result was the statement of the people.

> *Immediately he arose, took up the bed, and went out in the presence of them all, so that all were amazed and glorified God, saying, "We never saw anything like this!"*

The word *amazed* in this scripture is the Greek word *existemi*. It means "to put out of wits." These people were flabbergasted at what they were witnessing. They were utterly astounded by the display of power that was present with Jesus. The statement that came from this place of being awestruck was, *"We never saw anything like this."* This is where we are headed as a church and in our culture. There is coming a move of God the likes of which has not been seen. It will grasp the attention of the masses unlike anything before. It will be a demonstration of God's resurrection power that is birthing this foretold revival.

When we talk of revival, it is impossible to have it without the resurrection power of the Lord. In fact, I would say that revival is God's resurrection power on display. Of course, resurrection is when something that has been dead is brought back to life again. The very idea carries with it that the grief associated with loss is wonderfully removed. We began to live out Isaiah 61:3.

> *To console those who mourn in Zion, To give them beauty for ashes, The oil of joy for mourning, The garment of praise for the spirit of heaviness; That they may be called trees of righteousness, The planting of the Lord, that He may be glorified.*

This is testifying of a place of grief becoming a place of glory. It is a replacing of sorrow and pain with celebration and praise. This is the result of resurrection life and power.

I've often thought of what it must have been like when Mary and Martha were consumed with grief over the loss of Lazarus. Their beloved brother was now in the grave and everything had changed. They had a new normal thrust on them. Then, Jesus showed up and the resurrection power of the Lord was manifested. Lazarus was brought out of the tomb and back to life again. The unthinkable occurred. That which seemed to be lost forever was instantly restored through the power of God.

Can you imagine the elation and absolute joy that must have erupted within Mary's and Martha's heart? It is unimaginable. Yet this is what the resurrection glory of God can do. I do believe we will see this kind of power again. Jesus was clear and adamant that these kinds of miracles would be present as we walked as His disciples. John 14:12 shows Jesus promising that greater works would be the portion of those who were His.

> *Most assuredly, I say to you, he who believes in Me, the works that I do he will do also; and greater works than these he will do, because I go to My Father.*

Jesus going to the Father was a reference to the coming of the Holy Spirit with His empowerment. When Jesus went to the Father, He was given the Holy Spirit to pour out on us. This is according to Acts 2:33.

> *Therefore being exalted to the right hand of God, and having received from the Father the promise of*

the Holy Spirit, He poured out this which you now
see and hear.

The coming of the Holy Spirit on the Day of Pentecost
was the sign that Jesus had now taken His place at the
right hand of God. He was now positioned in His exalted
posture as Lord of All. The Holy Spirit was now sent
to us because everything that needed to be done legally
for the Holy Spirit to reside on us, with us, and in us
was accomplished. Until this time, the Holy Spirit could
not reside in us. The necessary work of cleansing that
would allow this had not been done. The Holy Spirit's
power of resurrection living in us as believers required
we be vessels cleansed by the blood of Jesus. We can see
this is the ceremonial cleansing that was required to
proclaim lepers free of leprosy. Leviticus 14:14-17 shows
the ritual followed to declare a previous leper free from
leprosy. Leprosy is considered a typology of sin. This is
why whoever had this dreaded disease had to cry out,
"Unclean, unclean!" should someone come near them.
This was a statement of defilement and impurity they
were forced to confess.

> *The priest shall take some of the blood of the trespass*
> *offering, and the priest shall put it on the tip of the*
> *right ear of him who is to be cleansed, on the thumb*
> *of his right hand, and on the big toe of his right foot.*
> *And the priest shall take some of the log of oil, and*

pour it into the palm of his own left hand. Then the priest shall dip his right finger in the oil that is in his left hand, and shall sprinkle some of the oil with his finger seven times before the Lord. And of the rest of the oil in his hand, the priest shall put some on the tip of the right ear of him who is to be cleansed, on the thumb of his right hand, and on the big toe of his right foot, on the blood of the trespass offering.

Notice that the priest who witnessed to the fact of the cleansing of the leper applied first the blood, then the oil. This is a prophetic picture of how we are cleansed and the empowerment we should receive. The blood that cleanses us is first applied. The blood purchases us and cleanses us. Colossians 1:14 clearly lets us know that the blood is what guarantees our forgiveness.

In whom we have redemption through His blood, the forgiveness of sins.

First Peter 1:18-19 says we are redeemed from everything that would claim ownership of us. Jesus' blood has reclaimed us as His own.

Knowing that you were not redeemed with corruptible things, like silver or gold, from your aimless conduct received by tradition from your fathers, but with the precious blood of Christ, as of a lamb without blemish and without spot.

The blood of the Lamb, Jesus, has legally purchased and cleansed us from all unrighteousness and sin. We no longer belong to the powers of darkness but now are the possession of the Lord. Notice that when the defilements and their legal claims are removed, then the oil was also applied. The priest would place the oil on top of the previously applied blood. This prophetic act was making a spiritual statement. It was proclaiming that *the Spirit can only anoint what the blood has cleansed*. Whatever the spirit anoints must first be cleansed by the blood. This is why we are told in the New Testament that we are sealed by the Holy Spirit. Ephesians 1:13 tells us that after we believed, which would be the moment and time when the blood cleansed us, the Holy Spirit then seals us.

> *In Him you also trusted, after you heard the word of truth, the gospel of your salvation; in whom also, having believed, you were sealed with the Holy Spirit of promise.*

The Holy Spirit of promise, or what the Father guaranteed those who were His, anoints us. The word *sealed* in the Greek is *sphragizo*. It means "to stamp for preservation and/or security." The Holy Spirit is assigned to protect and guard all that the blood has bought. The anointing of His presence comes upon any and all that belong to Him by the purchasing power of Jesus' blood. We can also see this idea in Exodus 30:30-33, which gives us some insight into the anointing oil that was fashioned at the instructions of God.

> *And you shall anoint Aaron and his sons, and consecrate them, that they may minister to Me as priests. And you shall speak to the children of Israel, saying: "This shall be a holy anointing oil to Me throughout your generations. It shall not be poured on man's flesh; nor shall you make any other like it, according to its composition. It is holy, and it shall be holy to you. Whoever compounds any like it, or whoever puts any of it on an outsider, shall be cut off from his people."*

There were several mandates associated with the application of the anointing oil. Notice, however, that the anointing oil was forbidden to be placed on an *outsider*. This meant that no one outside the covenant was allowed to be anointed. This is because the anointing oil was only for those within the covenant who had been bought, purchased, and cleansed by the blood. Anyone who truly belongs to Jesus will have the anointing of God on their life. If there is no anointing, then there should be an investigation to see whether one really belongs to the Lord or not. Whoever is His will be sealed with the Holy Spirit of promise.

The final thing I would mention here is that the blood and the oil were placed on the previous leper's right ear, right thumb, and right big toe. The significance of this is that we are cleansed and empowered to hear, work, and walk. The ear speaks of our hearing in the spirit realm. The thumb speaks of our empowerment to work and minister as we ought. The big toe speaks of our walk of purity and holiness before the Lord. The cleansing of the blood and the resulting empowerment of the Holy Spirit enables us to function in this realm of resurrected power. Romans 1:3-4 calls the Holy Spirit the *spirit of holiness.*

> *Concerning His Son Jesus Christ our Lord, who was born of the seed of David according to the flesh, and declared to be the Son of God with power according to the Spirit of holiness, by the resurrection from the dead.*

Jesus was declared to be the Son of God through the Holy Spirit by the resurrection from the dead. His resurrection testified of who He really is. This resurrection occurred by the power of the Holy Spirit dwelling with Him and in Him. We are told in Romans 8:11 that if this Spirit dwells in us, we too can and will experience this resurrection life.

> *But if the Spirit of Him who raised Jesus from the dead dwells in you, He who raised Christ from the dead will also give life to your mortal bodies through His Spirit who dwells in you.*

This Holy Spirit will empower us to experience and move in the power of His resurrection. We will see this occur as we make room for Him. That which the blood has legally cleansed, the Holy Spirit has now come to anoint and empower. We are called and commissioned to be those who function in resurrection power through the Holy Spirit of God. With this anointing of power and resurrection, we can see otherwise unchangeable things brought back to life. We can see what seems to be final and the fate of people overturned and life given back. This is because we serve a God of resurrection. The legal work of Jesus on the cross allows the empowerment of the Spirit of God to bring this resurrection power. Let's receive it and begin to manifest the glory of who Jesus is!

As I approach the Courts of Heaven, Lord, I ask for Your resurrection power to bring Your reviving work. I would remind this Court that when Jesus died on the cross every legal thing necessary to experience resurrection and revival was accomplished. I ask for the anointing of Your presence to now come to renew, restore, and redeem all things in me to Your purposes. From Your Courts, Lord, would You allow a fresh empowerment of Your Holy Spirit to manifest the same power that raised Jesus from the dead. In Jesus' Name, amen!

Chapter 2

THE COURTS OF HEAVEN, RESURRECTION, AND REVIVAL

So often, it would seem that we fall short of the glory of God and His resurrection life. We seem to live life outside the strength and power of this reviving force that clearly is to be ours. Yet as New Testament believers we are promised this power and glory. In John 11:25-26 as Jesus prepared to raise Lazarus from the dead, He made a monumental statement. He declared that whoever believes in Him will have resurrection life.

> Jesus said to her, "I am the resurrection and the life. He who believes in Me, though he may die, he shall live. And whoever lives and believes in Me shall never die. Do you believe this?"

What a declaration. If we are to take this at face value, which we should if we are His disciples and live by Him, we will not die. This is not speaking of a physical death. This is speaking of the fact that as believers we are to have His abundant life pulsating in us. Even in the face of physical death, we shall live. When we have Jesus, we have life. First John 5:11-12 shows that Jesus Himself is this life.

> *And this is the testimony: that God has given us eternal life, and this life is in His Son. He who has the Son has life; he who does not have the Son of God does not have life.*

The way to experience the resurrection life of Jesus is by having Him as the Son of God. It is impossible not to have the life of God when you have the Son. Resurrection life is not a result of gimmicks or formulas. Resurrection life comes from a living relationship with Jesus. It is interesting that the scripture uses the word *testimony* to clarify who has life and who doesn't have life. This is the Greek word *marturia*, and it means "judicial evidence given." This would mean that in a Court whoever has the Son would be deemed as one who has life. Eternal life in the present and in the eternities to come will be judicially established by who does or does not have the Son. If we are walking in a living relationship with Jesus, we have life now and also in the life to come. We have passed from death to life because of our connection and joining with Jesus. John 5:24 verifies this reality.

> *Most assuredly, I say to you, he who hears My word and believes in Him who sent Me has everlasting life,*

and shall not come into judgment, but has passed from death into life.

When we believe in Jesus and the One who sent Him, which is God the Father, we escape judgment and pass into life. The word *passed* is the Greek word *metabaino*. It means "to change place." When we accept Jesus as the Son and our Redeemer, we changed places in the spirit realm. We move from a place of condemnation and judgment to a place of redemption and life. This is not only a legal transition, but the Holy Spirit makes this a living reality in our lives. Let's petition the Court of Heaven for this.

> Lord, as I stand before Your Courts by faith, I request that all the Son has died for me to have would be mine. I ask that the legal work of Jesus for me on the cross would now become reality in my life. I declare before this Court that I have passed from death and condemnation to redemption and life. Let it be recorded that even as I have the Son, I have life now and also for all eternity. Let it be known before this Court that Jesus is my Savior and my Lord. In Jesus' Name, amen.

When we speak of having life that is a result of having Jesus as the Son living in us, we should be resonating with the abundant life of Jesus. John 10:10 tells us that Jesus came that we might have life and have it more abundantly.

The thief does not come except to steal, and to kill,
and to destroy. I have come that they may have life,
and that they may have it more abundantly.

Even though Jesus' purpose, desire, and intent is for us
to have life, the devil as the thief desires to destroy it all.
The Lord wants to replace every destructive thing with
His life and power in our lives. When we have the life of
God, we are victorious, abounding, healthy, prosperous,
and living in harmony with God and others. Every
promise made to us through Jesus and His work for us
on the cross is to progressively become ours. If this is true
then why do so many see more of the devouring work of
satan than the resurrection life of Jesus? Why is the thief
being so effective against so many people?

The answer is found in the legal rights that satan has
claimed against us. If we are to deal with these legal rights,
we must step into the Courts of Heaven and see satan's
voice of accusation against us revoked. Resurrection
life and revival will come at the expense of operating in
the Courts of Heaven. The delay of revival through the
resurrection power of God is not God withholding it. It is
the resistance of the devil based on legal claims against us.
Once these legal claims are answered and removed, the
revival and resurrection power we cry for will manifest.
Satan actually has cases against the church that are
stopping the passionate release of God in revival form.

Understanding the Courts of Heaven is critical to what I am describing. Daniel 7:9-10 is the clearest picture we have in Scriptures of the Courts of Heaven. Even though we can see these Courts in other places of Scripture, here they are the most evident.

> *I watched till thrones were put in place, And the Ancient of Days was seated; His garment was white as snow, And the hair of His head was like pure wool. His throne was a fiery flame, Its wheels a burning fire; A fiery stream issued And came forth from before Him. A thousand thousands ministered to Him; Ten thousand times ten thousand stood before Him. The court was seated, And the books were opened.*

Daniel, as a seer—that is, one who had the ability to see into the unseen world—witnessed a Court setting in heaven. He saw God as the Ancient of Days seated on His throne of judgment. He saw much more activity associated with this heavenly judicial system. Suffice it to say here, he saw the Court of Heaven seated and ready to hear cases presented. In Luke 18:1-8, Jesus would place prayer in a judicial setting as well. He would speak of an unjust judge refusing to render a just verdict for a widow.

> *Then He spoke a parable to them, that men always ought to pray and not lose heart, saying: "There was in a certain city a judge who did not fear God nor*

regard man. Now there was a widow in that city; and she came to him, saying, 'Get justice for me from my adversary.' And he would not for a while; but afterward he said within himself, 'Though I do not fear God nor regard man, yet because this widow troubles me I will avenge her, lest by her continual coming she weary me.'"

Then the Lord said, "Hear what the unjust judge said. And shall God not avenge His own elect who cry out day and night to Him, though He bears long with them? I tell you that He will avenge them speedily. Nevertheless, when the Son of Man comes, will He really find faith on the earth?"

This widow, through a persistent presentation of her case, saw this judicial system set a decision in place to stop her adversary from harming and hindering her. As I have said in my previous books on the Court of Heaven, Jesus is not saying God is an unjust Judge we have to convince. His point is, if this widow can get a verdict from an unjust Judge, how much more can we come before God as Judge of all and see Him render righteous verdicts on our behalf. Jesus set prayer into the Courts of Heaven that Daniel so gloriously saw generations before.

This Court is still active today. Just like with other places in the Spirit realm that we can tread, we have access into this place by the blood of Jesus. Hebrews 10:19-22 encourages us to take the place that has been granted to us by His blood.

> *Therefore, brethren, having boldness to enter the Holiest by the blood of Jesus, by a new and living way which He consecrated for us, through the veil, that is, His flesh, and having a High Priest over the house of God, let us draw near with a true heart in full assurance of faith, having our hearts sprinkled from an evil conscience and our bodies washed with pure water.*

The Holiest speaks of the innermost place of the sanctuary/temple/tabernacle that Moses erected. The high priest, one time a year, could enter this place to present the blood of the Passover lamb for the redemption of a nation. This was a picture of what Jesus would do for us with His own blood. The blood of those lambs, bulls, and goats was only sufficient to legally cleanse the nation and people for a year. Hebrews 10:1-14 shows that the offering of the Levitical priesthood was only a temporary fix to the sin of man. These offerings were designed to be a prophetic picture of what was to come, but also to keep the judgment of God off a nation until the fullness of Jesus' offering might be seen.

> *For the law, having a shadow of the good things to come, and not the very image of the things, can never with these same sacrifices, which they offer*

continually year by year, make those who approach perfect. For then would they not have ceased to be offered? For the worshipers, once purified, would have had no more consciousness of sins. But in those sacrifices there is a reminder of sins every year. For it is not possible that the blood of bulls and goats could take away sins.

Therefore, when He came into the world, He said:
"Sacrifice and offering You did not desire,
But a body You have prepared for Me.
In burnt offerings and sacrifices for sin
You had no pleasure.
Then I said, 'Behold, I have come—
In the volume of the book it is written of Me—
To do Your will, O God.'"

Previously saying, "Sacrifice and offering, burnt offerings, and offerings for sin You did not desire, nor had pleasure in them" (which are offered according to the law), then He said, "Behold, I have come to do Your will, O God." He takes away the first that He may establish the second. By that will we have been sanctified through the offering of the body of Jesus Christ once for all.

And every priest stands ministering daily and offering repeatedly the same sacrifices, which can never take away sins. But this Man, after He had offered one

> *sacrifice for sins forever, sat down at the right hand of God, from that time waiting till His enemies are made His footstool. For by one offering He has perfected forever those who are being sanctified.*

When Jesus died on the cross, took His own blood into the Holiest of Holies, and offered it there, all that was needed was now done. There is not another sacrifice required for our forgiveness, redemption, and justification. We stand complete in Jesus as our perfect atonement in answer to our every need. Jesus as our High Priest doesn't enter once every year to provide this atonement. He stands perpetually before the Lord on our behalf as our Intercessor. This is one of His functions as our High Priest. Hebrews 7:25 tells us this intercession is for the purpose of us being saved to the *uttermost*.

> *Therefore He is also able to save to the uttermost those who come to God through Him, since He always lives to make intercession for them.*

Jesus, from this place He is now functioning in, is praying into reality all that He died for us to have. This means He is seeking to move us into a full expression and experience in His resurrection and revival power. His desire is for us to have life and have it more abundantly. This is really what the Court of Heaven is about. I am seeking to get into place the full benefit of everything Jesus died for me to have. We know that even though Jesus has stripped satan of his legal rights, he still tries to use them against us. Peter in First Peter 5:8 tells us that satan is operating as our legal opponent still.

Be sober, be vigilant; because your adversary the devil walks about like a roaring lion, seeking whom he may devour.

The word adversary is the Greek word antidikos. This word means "a legal opponent." It comes from two words, anti and dikos. Anti means "against or instead of." Dikos means "rights." So the purpose of the devil as our legal opponent is to deny us what is rightfully ours. Healing, breakthrough, prosperity, family order, and all other benefits of salvation belong to us through covenant with Jesus. However, the devil is building cases against us as our adversary/*antidikos* to deny us what is ours. This means we must go into the Courts of Heaven and present cases based on what Jesus has done for us. When we do this, we get the full benefit of all Jesus has died for us to have. Now it is not just principles, but we actually possess that which is ours because of Jesus and His blood. We actually get the full effect of having passed from death to life. We get the full effect of having abundant life. We get the full effect of resurrection power flowing in us. We get the full effect of His reviving strength. This is because whatever case the devil is bringing to hinder and deny these realities is removed from the Courts of Heaven.

One of the main things to getting decisions in place from the Courts of Heaven is silencing voices. Isaiah 54:17 refers to these voices that can make causes against us.

> *"No weapon formed against you shall prosper, And every tongue which rises against you in judgment You shall condemn. This is the heritage of the servants of the Lord, And their righteousness is from Me," says the Lord.*

We are confidently told that "no weapon" will prosper that might be formed against us. The weapon could be a curse that results in sickness, poverty, destruction, or limitations and restrictions on our lives. It could be family devastation or any other negative life altering thing that would seek to touch us. Notice, however, that the solution to any "weapon" against us is to condemn or silence the "tongue" that rises in judgment. We see therefore that the real thing we need to deal with is the "tongue" or "voice" that is allowing the weapon to operate. Often we are trying to stop the destructive force of the weapon. However, if we can silence the tongue and voice in the spirit world, the weapon will cease to operate!

I am convinced that anything that we fight against that is against us is driven by a voice or tongue making a case against us in the unseen realm. This is what happened to Job. Job went into terrible tragedy and trauma in his life. It would have appeared from the natural perspective that things just befell him. However, we know by looking at the behind the scenes activity that it was the voice of satan against him that produced this. Job 1:8-12 reveals this.

> *Then the Lord said to Satan, "Have you considered My servant Job, that there is none like him on the earth, a blameless and upright man, one who fears God and shuns evil?"*
>
> *So Satan answered the Lord and said, "Does Job fear God for nothing? Have You not made a hedge around him, around his household, and around all that he has on every side? You have blessed the work of his hands, and his possessions have increased in the land. But now, stretch out Your hand and touch all that he has, and he will surely curse You to Your face!"*
>
> *And the Lord said to Satan, "Behold, all that he has is in your power; only do not lay a hand on his person."*
>
> *So Satan went out from the presence of the Lord.*

We know that destruction began to hit the house of Job because of the devil's voice against him. The dialogue between God and satan in the unseen realm is what precipitated and even caused this destruction. We see this later also in Job 2:3-7 when satan again, through accusation, brings words against Job.

Then the Lord said to Satan, "Have you considered My servant Job, that there is none like him on the earth, a blameless and upright man, one who fears God and shuns evil? And still he holds fast to his integrity, although you incited Me against him, to destroy him without cause."

So Satan answered the Lord and said, "Skin for skin! Yes, all that a man has he will give for his life. But stretch out Your hand now, and touch his bone and his flesh, and he will surely curse You to Your face!"

And the Lord said to Satan, "Behold, he is in your hand, but spare his life."

So Satan went out from the presence of the Lord, and struck Job with painful boils from the sole of his foot to the crown of his head.

The first word against Job caused great devastation to touch his wealth and family. The second word against him caused sickness and disease to come on Job himself. My main point, however, is that the "weapons" working against Job were a result of the accusations rendered against him. I'm sure that Job was completely unaware of the cause of his tragedies. Yet it was the voice against him in the unseen world that caused it.

If we can be aware of these voices and stop these voices of accusation, we can stop the weapons! By the way, the word *judgment* in Isaiah 54:17 is the Hebrew word *mishpat*.

It means "a verdict pronounced judicially." This means that the voices or tongues against us can result in verdicts or sentences coming upon us. This is exactly what happened to Job. A sentence was passed down upon Job because of the voices in the unseen world against him. To stop the sentence we could be living out and experience instead resurrection life and power, we must silence these voices. Revelation 12:10-11 tells us some of the process of doing this from a Court of Heaven perspective.

Then I heard a loud voice saying in heaven, "Now salvation, and strength, and the kingdom of our God, and the power of His Christ have come, for the accuser of our brethren, who accused them before our God day and night, has been cast down. And they overcame him by the blood of the Lamb and by the word of their testimony, and they did not love their lives to the death.

The word *accuser* is the Greek word *kategoros*. It means "against one in the assembly, a complainant at law." The accuser of the brothers is therefore not someone speaking evil against you in the natural world. It is something in the spirit realm making a case against you in the Courts of Heaven. These are voices that must be silenced. We silence these voices by the blood of the Lamb, the word of our testimony, and not loving our lives unto death. These three functions in the Courts of Heaven will cause the voices against us to be condemned and not able to fashion weapons against us. The blood of the Lamb is what we use to dismiss whatever is claiming a legal right against us. Hebrews 12:24 tells us that Jesus' blood, the blood of sprinkling, is speaking for us.

> *To Jesus the Mediator of the new covenant, and to the blood of sprinkling that speaks better things than that of Abel.*

We need to repent and come into an agreement with what this blood is saying for us. The blood of Abel cried out for judgment against Cain (see Gen. 4:9). The blood of Jesus, however, is crying for mercy, forgiveness, and redemption for us. This blood speaking before the Courts of Heaven grants God the legal right to redeem us from every destructive thing speaking against us. This blood speaking for us annuls the voices against us in the spirit realm as we accept and agree with it. However, the one thing I would mention is that we must repent. Repentance is essential to benefiting from the voice of the blood. First John 1:7 tells us we must come out of darkness and into light to be cleansed by the blood of the Lamb.

> *But if we walk in the light as He is in the light, we have fellowship with one another, and the blood of Jesus Christ His Son cleanses us from all sin.*

Walking in the light does not mean sinless living. It means honest living. In other words we are bringing things out of darkness and hiding, repenting, and asking for forgiveness. This is walking in the light as He is in the light. When we do this, the blood speaks for us and erases the voices against us. Here's a prayer we can use for this:

> Lord, as I stand before You in Your Courts, I come out of darkness and into light. I acknowledge my sin before You. Against You and You alone have I sinned. I ask, Lord, that Your blood might speak for me right now. May Your blood silence every voice speaking against me that is taking opportunity by my sin. I ask that these voices be silenced and may Your blood deliver me from their desired destruction against me. In Jesus' Name, amen.

Another thing we use in the Courts is the *word of our testimony*. Just as the blood speaks and dismisses cases against us, the word of our testimony presents cases on our behalf. In any real Court system, we need not just cases and voices against us dismissed, but also cases presented for us. The word of our testimony accomplishes this. This is why we are told in Isaiah 43:26 to bring God into remembrance.

> *Put Me in remembrance; Let us contend together;*
> *State your case, that you may be acquitted.*

We put God into remembrance by the word of our testimony. We tell God what He has promised, what is written in the books of heaven about us, and what Jesus has done for us legally. By all of these means, we bring the word of our testimony before the Lord in His Courts. The result is we are acquitted or justified of any condemning thing. We are presenting evidence before Him concerning our destiny, future, and breakthroughs. The result will be God-granted rights to render decisions from His Court in our favor. Here is a prayer designed to help in this process:

> As I come before Your Courts, Lord, thank You for any and every case against me that Your blood has silenced. I now present a case on my behalf as the word of my testimony. I call You into remembrance of that which You wrote in my book before time began. I ask You, Lord, for my prophetic destiny to come to pass. Lord, allow all that is rightfully mine from You to be seen and manifest. In Jesus' Name, amen.

As you present your word of testimony, be a specific as you can with revelation you have received from the Lord. What He has shown you concerning your destiny and future, request this from Him. This is part of presenting your case before His Courts.

The final thing spoken of is the laying down of our lives. The Scriptures say that those who overcame the effects of the accuser and his voice loved not their lives unto death. This means there was no sacrifice too big that they weren't willing to make for God's kingdom and purpose. It is the laying down of our lives that grants us tremendous places of authority in the Courts of Heaven. When we say yes to the Lord and choose His will and way over our own desire, it is recorded in heaven. Whoever will do this will have a status in heaven from which they function. The Bible tells us in Hebrews 11:39 that people of faith who made great sacrifices have a good report or testimony in heaven.

And all these, having obtained a good testimony through faith, did not receive the promise.

Even though they didn't get the fullness of the promise while alive in the earth, they did obtain a good testimony or witness about themselves in heaven. This means they carry an authority before the Lord and His Courts. This allows them to petition the Court for themselves and others with great effectiveness. The more we allow the Holy Spirit to claim us for the purposes of God, the greater our realm of influence will be in the heavenly realm. You do not have to die to have this influence. You can have it now, as you step into and function in the Courts. You may plead with the Courts for resurrection life to flow and His reviving power to be known. Here is an additional prayer to request this before God:

As I approach Your Courts, Lord, I ask that I might lay my life down in agreement with

Your will. Lord, allow me the privilege of submitting my life to You, that Your will could be accomplished. From this place of surrender, may my words carry authority and weight in Your Courts. Thank You, Lord, for hearing me and responding to my cry. May I be a part of praying into reality Your desire and passion in the earth. In Jesus' Name, amen.

CHAPTER 3

JESUS' LEGAL WORK

If we are to operate in resurrection power from the Courts of Heaven, we must understand the legal relevance of Jesus' activities on our behalf. This includes His death, His burial, His resurrection, and His ascension. We must know how to take what He has legally done and present it as evidence in the Court of Heaven that it might speak for us. One of the greatest joys of my heart is presenting evidence in the Courts of Heaven based on Jesus' atoning work. All that was done in regard to these things was legal in nature. Through His death He legally judged sin, sickness, poverty, disease, and any other thing against us. Remember that Romans 8:3 tells us that Jesus condemned sin in the flesh.

> *For what the law could not do in that it was weak through the flesh, God did by sending His own Son in the likeness of sinful flesh, on account of sin: He condemned sin in the flesh.*

The word *condemned* is the Greek word *katakrino*. It means "to judge against, to sentence." Jesus' activities in the midst of His suffering legally made all that was against us illegal. His legal activity made this powerless to effect and determine our life and our future. However, the effects of this must be set in place in the Courts of Heaven. Any verdict rendered from the cross of Jesus must be executed into place. This is why we come before the Courts of Heaven and present the work of Jesus as evidence on our behalf. This is one of the things we so often don't do as New Testament believers. We don't aggressively set these things in place to speak for us. When we read certain scriptures in the New Testament and even in the Old, they are the *stated verdicts* from the cross of Jesus. For instance, Colossians 2:14 declares anything against us was proclaimed illegal at the cross.

Having wiped out the handwriting of requirements that was against us, which was contrary to us. And He has taken it out of the way, having nailed it to the cross.

Jesus *legally* revoked all accusations against us. He caused them to be non-effective through His sacrifice. Many times, I take these words into the Courts and ask that any voice coming against me would now be silenced. Just because there is a verdict in place for me doesn't mean voices will not try to speak in the spirit world against me. I must present as evidence that which Jesus has done. Another scripture that should be presented is Galatians 3:13.

> *Christ has redeemed us from the curse of the law, having become a curse for us (for it is written, "Cursed is everyone who hangs on a tree").*

This is all legal language. Jesus, as the sinless, unadulterated Son of God, offered Himself for us. He took our place on the cross and took the curse. Remember, He became sin for us, that we might be the righteousness of God in Him. This is according to Second Corinthians 5:21.

> *For He made Him who knew no sin to be sin for us, that we might become the righteousness of God in Him.*

This again is legal verbiage designed to awaken in us the reality of what Jesus has accomplished. All this and so much more was done because of Jesus' suffering and brutal treatment at the hands of sinners and the devil. He suffered so much that we might have the legal things necessary to live an abundant life of resurrection. Let me help us take these things and present them before the Lord and His Courts.

> As I come before Your Courts, my Lord, thank You so much for what You have done through Your sacrifice for me. I ask on the basis of Your

offering for me according to Colossians 2:14 that any and all charges would be dropped. I asked that all condemnation, guilt, shame, and unworthiness would be revoked from my life. Any penalty for sin, I say, has been paid by You. I ask, because You have nailed these words against me to the cross, that the voices speaking against me, causing these issues of shame, would now be silenced. Let what You did for me now speak on my behalf before Your Courts in Jesus' Name!

I thank You that according to Galatians 3:13 all curses against me have been removed. You, Lord, became a curse for me. You took on Yourself all that was meant for me. You legally set me free when You suffered and died on the cross. Now, Lord, let this speak for me today in Jesus' Name. Let any and all effects of curses against me, my body, my finances, my family, and any other realm now be declared to be illegal and unrighteous. It must be gone in Jesus' Name.

Thank You, Lord, as I stand in Your Courts that You became sin for me that I might be Your righteousness. I therefore have righteous standing before You. Thank You for Your legal activity on the cross that set this is place. I can stand before You without fear because of Your perfect, legal work on my behalf. By faith I receive from You all that You did for me. May Your Holy Spirit now bring into reality all that You died for me to have. Thank You for the Spirit that is my legal aid to bring me into all that You have legally accomplished. In Jesus' Name, amen.

In addition to Jesus' suffering, sacrifice, and atoning work for us through His death, He also accomplished much by His resurrection. Through His death He took on Himself legally the penalty for my sin. Through His resurrection, however, I am raised with Him into a newness of life. This also is a legal accomplishment. Romans 6:5-11 gives us some astounding insight into what legally happened for us at not only Jesus' death but also His resurrection.

For if we have been united together in the likeness of His death, certainly we also shall be in the likeness of His resurrection, knowing this, that our old man was crucified with Him, that the body of sin might be done away with, that we should no longer be slaves of sin. For he who has died has been freed from sin. Now if we died with Christ, we believe that we shall also live with Him, knowing that Christ, having been raised from the dead, dies no more. Death no longer has dominion over Him. For the death that He died, He died to sin once for all; but the life that

*He lives, He lives to God. Likewise you also, reckon
yourselves to be dead indeed to sin, but alive to God
in Christ Jesus our Lord.*

Baptism is a means by which we literally lay hold of
what was legally done. When we are baptized in water, we
legally identify with His death, but also legally identify with
His resurrection and life. Just like the life Jesus presently
lives is a result of His resurrection, we through faith
reckon all this into place. We acknowledge and embrace
His legal work for us. The Holy Spirit then takes the legal
significance of His resurrection and brings that eternal life
into us! This means that what might have tried to cling to
us from the old is removed as we enter into the new. It has
no place in our new experienced as the raised of the Lord.
We are told in Colossians 3:1-4 that our experience in His
resurrection changes our passions and desires.

*If then you were raised with Christ, seek those things
which are above, where Christ is, sitting at the right
hand of God. Set your mind on things above, not on
things on the earth. For you died, and your life is
hidden with Christ in God. When Christ who is our
life appears, then you also will appear with Him in
glory.*

As a result of our legal raising into His newness of life,
our hearts should be turned toward seeking Him. Instead
of an interest in the earthly realm, our passions are on

Him and what is above. This is why carnal believers have never actually understood what happened to them at salvation. If we are truly born again, there should be some interest and desire toward what is heavenly and not just earthly. That part of us that is interested only in earthly things legally died with Jesus. That part of us that desires God—His gifts, His passions, His longings—came alive because of Jesus' resurrection. We also have a desire to enter into all that we really are. This will happen when we see Jesus. The full manifestation of who we are will be see when we physically see Jesus in His glory. Who we are in the resurrected life of Jesus will be revealed. This is all because of what was accomplished at Jesus' resurrection.

> Thank You so much, Lord, for Your resurrection and new realm of life legally obtained for us. I thank You that because of Your resurrection there is a cry for me in Your Courts for newness of life. I thank You that anything that would try to cling to me from the old has lost the power to legally do so. Through my water baptism, I thank You that this is set in place. My old man (old sin nature) died with You and the new man has risen with You. Thank You that there is a new set of passions in me for the heavenly. Thank You that my heart is no longer set on the earthly, but I yearn for the new and heavenly realm. I thank You that I also look forward to

the day when the fullness of who I am in Your resurrection is made manifest. Lord, when You appear I will also appear in Your glory with You. Thank You for all that Your resurrection has done and for the Holy Spirit who brings into reality all that has been legally obtained for me. In Jesus' Name, amen.

There is one more aspect to what Jesus legally accomplished and that is His ascension. Just like His death and resurrection set things legally in place for us, His ascension accomplished legal issues as well. The main thing legally accomplished was the right to release the Holy Spirit to us. The Bible stated in Acts 2:31-33 that when Jesus ascended and sat down with the Father that the Holy Spirit was given to Him to pour out on us.

He, foreseeing this, spoke concerning the resurrection of the Christ, that His soul was not left in Hades, nor did His flesh see corruption. This Jesus God has raised up, of which we are all witnesses. Therefore being exalted to the right hand of God, and having received from the Father the promise of the Holy Spirit, He poured out this which you now see and hear.

As Jesus was resurrected and took His place with the Father, this allowed the Father to legally give the Holy Spirit to Jesus. He then poured the Holy Spirit out on those in the upper room. Yet not just those but us as well. The legal work of Jesus in His death, burial, resurrection, and then ascension caused the Holy Spirit to be poured out on us. One of the aspects to this was the Holy Spirit came to dwell in us and not just on us or with us. John 14:17 tells us this wonderful truth.

> *The Spirit of truth, whom the world cannot receive, because it neither sees Him nor knows Him; but you know Him, for He dwells with you and will be in you.*

Up until this point, the Spirit had anointed people but never really been in them. This is because we had never legally been cleansed so that we could be a suitable dwelling place for Him. However, the blood has so sufficiently cleansed us that we can now see the Spirit dwell in us. The blood of bulls and goats was not sufficient for cleansing us. However, when Jesus gave Himself as *the Sacrifice*, what legally and functionally was done allowed the Spirit of God to inhabit us as consecrated vessels to Him. Everything was now legally in place for the Spirit of God to take up residence in us. We should claim this before the Courts of Heaven and accept the anointing and presence of the Spirit of God into our lives.

> Lord, as I stand before Your Courts, I remind these Courts of all that You have done on the cross, in Your burial, through Your resurrection,

and in Your ascension. Thank You that You have now sat down at the Father's right hand. As a result of all this legal activity, I now ask for a fresh empowerment of Your Spirit. I receive Your anointing and presence into my life. Even as You poured out the Spirit You received from the Father, let this Holy Spirit now come into my life. Let Your presence be with me, on me, and in me. Come, Holy Spirit, and take up residence in my heart now, in Jesus' Name, amen.

CHAPTER 4

WHO IS YOUR GOD?

As we contend from the Courts of Heaven for the resurrected life of Jesus to birth revival, we need to make sure we have a God who does such things. Abraham and Sarah experienced the resurrection life of God when their ability to conceive and birth Isaac was enacted. Of course there had been decades of barrenness, hope deferred, and seemingly a resignation of their childless lot in life. When we read the New Testament version of Abraham and Sarah, you would think they never had a doubt concerning what would happen. However, when we read the Old Testament accounts, we see that Abraham and Sarah were very much human and did in fact struggle with unbelief. We see both of them coming to a place of hope deferred, or devastating discouragement. We see this in Abraham in Genesis 17:15-19. He actually asked God to just let Ishmael be the one the promise was fulfilled through.

Then God said to Abraham, "As for Sarai your wife, you shall not call her name Sarai, but Sarah shall be her name. And I will bless her and also give you a son by her; then I will bless her, and she shall be a mother of nations; kings of peoples shall be from her."

Then Abraham fell on his face and laughed, and said in his heart, "Shall a child be born to a man who is one hundred years old? And shall Sarah, who is ninety years old, bear a child?" And Abraham said to God, "Oh, that Ishmael might live before You!"

Then God said: "No, Sarah your wife shall bear you a son, and you shall call his name Isaac; I will establish My covenant with him for an everlasting covenant, and with his descendants after him."

The Lord told Abraham "No" at his request to acknowledge Ishmael. Remember that Ishmael was born as a result of Abraham and Sarah seeking to have children in their house. Sarah had given Hagar, her handmaiden, to Abraham to seek to raise up children because she was barren. This caused great conflict in the home. Eventually, Sarah demanded of Abraham that Hagar and her son Ishmael would be sent away. This was a very grievous thing to Abraham. He clearly loved Ishmael. However, he was not the chosen seed through whom God would bring His promise to Abraham.

This is a very clear picture of how we too can operate when the promises of God are slower in manifesting than we like. We can concoct and come up with plans that "help"

God out. However, all Abraham's and Sarah's plan did was bring confusion into their home and for generations and ages to come. The conflict in the Middle East today is a direct result of the *seeds* of Abraham warring with each other. This can be traced back to Abraham and Sarah's effort to birth in the flesh the promises of God that can only come through the Spirit of the Lord.

This is a lesson to us today. I have been guilty of giving birth to *things* that were not of the Spirit. They were good ideas, plans, and concepts that would have been deemed appropriate. The problem was they were of the flesh and not the Spirit. These things have always added a burden to me once they were operational. As a result of giving birth to them, I had to then take care of them. I had to financially care for them. I had to care for them with manpower/employees. I had to care for them with effort and attention that I could have been placing elsewhere. They have always brought confusion and stress into my life. Hopefully I have learned through the years to only *birth* what I sincerely feel is from the Lord. This makes life so much more joyful and painless.

The main reason we give birth to *Ishmaels* is because of our impatience. My impatience in waiting for and contending for the promises of God can cause me to birth things that are not from God. They may be *good* things, but they are not *God* things. Years ago I had a dream that characterizes this idea. It was a defining dream and word from God to me at that particular juncture in my life. In this particular season of my life, I was desiring to enter into what I knew was the destiny of God for my life. I wanted my own ministry and even church instead of serving where God had placed me. I was very impatient. In the dream, I was on a road leading up a mountain. The road was under construction, with much heavy machinery doing the work. I now know this was the Lord letting me know that everything was being arranged in me and for me to enter my destiny, but I needed to wait. The machinery was moving at a very slow pace. They were building the road; however, it seemed like it would take a long time. As a result of this slow movement, I decided to go around the machinery and get on my way.

I saw an opening between some of the equipment and the edge of the mountain cliff. I thought there was enough room to squeeze by. As I endeavored to do this, my foot slipped and I fell off the side of the mountain. I was hanging over the cliff from my armpits. As I was dangling in this precarious position, I realized that one of my sons, Adam, was hanging on my back. I remember in the dream feeling his little arms around my neck and his knees digging into my sides. At the time of this dream Adam would have been two years old or thereabouts. So here I am in this position, and suddenly I realized that my son/generations were in jeopardy.

As I was hanging there, I became aware of a man with a pickaxe who was diligently working on the road. I cried to him and said, "Please get Adam." Even though I was suspended in this place I was much more concerned about Adam losing his grip and falling than me. I wanted him lifted to safety and then myself brought out of this dangerous predicament. Instead, the man with the pickaxe (whom I understood to be the Holy Spirit) reached down and with supernatural strength picked me up with Adam still attached to my back. He set me down on solid ground in safety. He then spoke things to me. He first said, *"Many people have fallen to their destruction right here."*

Wow! In an effort to move quicker and at a faster pace than God, destruction can come. We must be willing to *wait on the Lord*. We have to allow the constructing business of God to happen in our lives. We have to let Him prepare us, but also prepare the way for us. The second thing this man said to me was, *"And if I have you, I have Adam."* The Lord was letting me know that as long as I followed Him and obeyed Him, Adam and the other children would do so as well. My yielded place before the Lord would allow not only God's purposes to be done in my life but also in my children and the generations to come. Remember that our God is a covenant keeping God even unto a thousand generations. Psalm 105:8 clearly makes this statement.

> *He remembers His covenant forever, The word which He commanded, for a thousand generations.*

From this scripture we can surmise that God keeping His covenant for a thousand generations is just a way of saying it is forever. If we know how to go into the Courts of Heaven, we can make demands on covenants that have been made in our generations. Often, we deal with the unrighteous aspect of demon contracts and covenants from our ancestry. This is necessary. However, we mustn't forget that we should make claims before the Courts of Heaven concerning righteous covenants made that are still intact in our bloodline. These can be very powerful and forceful petitions before the Court of Heaven.

As a result of this dream, I purposed in my heart to never move faster than God was moving. I purposed not to birth Ishmaels that would bring confusion and even destruction to my life and generations. I can say at this writing that we have seen and do continue to see blessings on our children. Adam is serving the Lord as a very successful pastor. My other children are living out their destinies and futures as well. My oldest son is in the business world. All the other five children and their spouses are in full-time ministry. God has surely blessed us. However, I could have messed it all up by trying to move at a quicker pace than ordained by God. Not only would my purpose and destiny have been forfeit, but potentially that of my generations as well. God is faithful to keep His word if we will just contend and wait on Him and His promises.

If you have been guilty of getting out of the timing of God, here is a prayer that you can pray:

> As I approach Your Courts, Lord, I acknowledge my impatience and tendency to run ahead of You. I ask that You be merciful to any place I've not waited on You. I ask that You help me to correct any destructive thing I might have caused by my insensitivity to Your leading. May Your mercy rule over me. May I find favor in Your sight as I seek to discern Your heart and timing and wait on You. May this be recorded before Your Courts as I accept Your resurrection power to restore and rebuild anything that might have been destroyed. In Jesus' Name, amen.

Abraham's desire for Ishmael to be recognized before the Lord was a result of hope deferred. This means usually a series of disappointments that has created a faithlessness in our hearts. Proverbs 13:12 shows this word from scripture.

> *Hope deferred makes the heart sick, when the desire comes, it is a tree of life.*

Hope deferred means that discouragement has come so often that we no longer have vibrant faith operating in us. It is now too painful to endeavor to believe again. We have shifted into survival mode. This is a safer place to live from. The problem is, in this place none of the promises of God can be fulfilled. It take real faith, willing to lay our lives down and believe God to see His promises fulfilled. This is the statement and testimony of scripture in Hebrews 11:8 and 11. We see Scripture mentioning Abraham and Sarah and the real faith they operated in to get the promises.

> By faith Abraham obeyed when he was called to go out to the place which he would receive as an inheritance. And he went out, not knowing where he was going.
>
> By faith Sarah herself also received strength to conceive seed, and she bore a child when she was past the age, because she judged Him faithful who had promised.

Real faith was present in both Abraham and Sarah to see the promises of God accomplished. However, this was not without them walking through times of hope deferred. We saw this in Abraham's life in the previous scriptures we mentioned. He struggled and desired Ishmael to be *the seed*. It was easier and required no faith for that to occur. However, God brought Abraham out of the hope deferred place and into real faith to believe again.

Sarah was struggling herself. This is why it says Sarah *received strength to conceive*. Before God could do a miracle of resurrection in both Abraham and Sarah's bodies, He had to revive their souls with real faith! Remember that when God showed up in Genesis 18:10-15, Sarah's hope deferred was revealed. She had given up any sense that she would have a baby. Her body no longer would allow this. She had passed the age of child bearing. What she had hoped and believed was not over. They were going to encounter the God of resurrection.

> *And He said, "I will certainly return to you according to the time of life, and behold, Sarah your wife shall have a son."*
>
> *(Sarah was listening in the tent door which was behind him.) Now Abraham and Sarah were old, well advanced in age; and Sarah had passed the age of childbearing. Therefore Sarah laughed within herself, saying, "After I have grown old, shall I have pleasure, my lord being old also?"*
>
> *And the Lord said to Abraham, "Why did Sarah laugh, saying, 'Shall I surely bear a child, since I am old?' Is anything too hard for the Lord? At the appointed time I will return to you, according to the time of life, and Sarah shall have a son."*
>
> *But Sarah denied it, saying, "I did not laugh," for she was afraid.*
>
> *And He said, "No, but you did laugh!"*

The Lord needed both Abraham and Sarah to be people of faith. It wasn't enough that Abraham had come out of hope deferred and back into faith. The Lord now needed Sarah to believe Him as well. When Sarah heard the promise that her body would be restored and resurrected, she laughed a laugh of unbelief. This laugh probably contained a sense of mockery, scorn, and pain from all the years of waiting. It was a laugh whose statement was, "*This is preposterous.*"

However, the Lord in His mercy confronted Sarah's unbelief and hope-deferred state. When she laughed, then denied it, God in essence said, "*Oh yes you did!*" This wasn't hard or calloused toward the journey Sarah had been on. It was to force her to acknowledge and deal with the state of her heart. Obviously, she did. She received strength to conceive.

Again, before their bodies could be revived, they had to first experience resurrection in their souls. The Lord in His graciousness and covenant keeping nature worked to fulfill this. The Lord's commitment to His covenant with us causes Him to continue even when we give up. This is what happened to Abraham and Sarah. This is why, according to Romans 4:17, Abraham was able to see the resurrection power of God move through himself and Sarah. This allowed the promise God had made them to be fulfilled. Let's look at this scripture again.

> (*As it is written, "I have made you a father of many nations") in the presence of Him whom he believed—God, who gives life to the dead and calls those things which do not exist as though they did.*

Allow me to show you four things connected to the resurrection power of God that flowed through Abraham and Sarah.

First of all, this was based on what God had said. Notice that the Lord previously had told Abraham, "*I have made you a father of many nations.*" This was one of several words that the Lord spoke to Abraham. These words were what kept Abraham alive with faith. This is because according to Romans 10:17 faith is a result of the word we have heard from the Lord.

> *So then faith comes by hearing, and hearing by the word of God.*

Notice that God says, "I have *made* you a father of many nations. He didn't say, "I am going to *make* you a father of many nations." There are many ideas about why the Lord speaks in such ways. One of them is because He is referring to what He wrote in a book in heaven about you. Psalm 139:16 shows that we have books in heaven that chronicle our destiny and future intended by God.

> *Your eyes saw my substance, being yet unformed. And in Your book they all were written, The days fashioned for me, When as yet there were none of them.*

In writing these words, David had an understanding that before time began, what I was supposed to do was established. This was a statement of the purpose and intent for David's life. Second Timothy 1:9 gives us more insight to this idea.

> Who has saved us and called us with a holy calling, not according to our works, but according to His own purpose and grace which was given to us in Christ Jesus before time began.

Notice that *purpose and grace* were given to us *before time began.* This means that what we are supposed to do was mandated before anything ever existed. The sun, moon, and stars determine time; therefore, before any of this existed my purpose was appointed me and grace was apportioned for me to fulfill it. It has been waiting for me to show up and discover what has already been granted to me. This was all written in a book before time began. Ephesians 2:10 makes another significant statement.

> For we are His workmanship, created in Christ Jesus for good works, which God prepared beforehand that we should walk in them.

The good works we are to perform have been prepared *beforehand.* Those things we are to walk in, our destiny and purpose, were set in place and recorded in a book before time began. This is why in Daniel 7:10 we see the Court of Heaven seated and the *books of destiny opened.*

A fiery stream issued And came forth from before Him. A thousand thousands ministered to Him; Ten thousand times ten thousand stood before Him. The court was seated, And the books were opened.

The books being opened means that the cases being presented in the Courts of Heaven come from these books. These books are the prophetic destiny and purpose for which we exist. When the Lord said to Abraham, "*I have made you a father of many nations,*" He spoke this way because it was written and established in the books of destiny in heaven.

We should take these kinds of words we have heard and petition the Courts of Heaven with them. This is what we discussed earlier concerning bringing God into remembrance. In other words, when we petition the Courts with what God has said and call Him into remembrance, it is a part of us being qualified to have what was determined before time began. So if we are to experience the resurrected life of God as Abraham and Sarah did, we must call into remembrance the word spoken out of the books of heaven concerning us. Allow it to birth faith as we present it as evidence before His Courts.

As I stand in Your Courts, Lord, I thank You that my destiny and the destiny of my family is written in Your book according to Psalm 139:16.

From this book, I prophetically sense and petition Your Court for this to be my reality. May all that is written in this book be known and fleshed out in my life. I request, Lord, that any and all accusations against me that would deny me this prophetic destiny now be silenced by the blood of Jesus speaking for me according to Hebrews 12:24.

A second thing we are told is that Abraham believed who he perceived God to be in *His presence*. This portion of Scripture in Romans 4:17 says, "*in the presence of whom he believed, God.*" The power to believe God is connected to walking in His presence. His presence creates atmosphere where spiritual activities are much easier. If we are to be people of faith who can receive from the Lord, we should cultivate the presence of the Lord.

I remember when God first called me to pray. There seemed to be no presence and no real unction to pray from. However, the longer I was faithful to *show up* and seek His face on a consistent basis, the more the closeness of the Lord would manifest. In this manifest presence, faith to believe God arises. His presence creates an atmosphere where the resurrection life of God can revive us. Wherever He is, there is life. Pray this prayer from the Courts of Heaven. One of the things that allows God's presence and closeness with us is found in Psalm 34:18.

The Lord is near to those who have a broken heart,
And saves such as have a contrite spirit.

A broken heart is not necessarily one that has been wounded or devastated. A broken and contrite person is one who has had their will submitted to the Lord. As they have sought the Lord, every place in them desiring their own way becomes surrendered to the Lord. These are those who are of a broken heart and contrite spirit. The Lord draws near to these. We can see this in Mary, who brought the alabaster box and broke it over the feet of Jesus in John 12:3. As they were celebrating the resurrection of Lazarus, Mary took what was very costly, as much as a year's wage, and anointed the feet of Jesus:

Then Mary took a pound of very costly oil of
spikenard, anointed the feet of Jesus, and wiped His
feet with her hair. And the house was filled with the
fragrance of the oil.

Notice that the fragrance filled the whole house. Anytime there is sacrifice made from a heart of brokenness and contriteness, the anointing of His presence will fill the house. His presence is almost always a result of someone flowing in brokenness before Him. As His presence comes, the resurrection life of Jesus will be revealed. This is what caused resurrection to happen with Abraham and Sarah—their bodies were renewed and reempowered because of God's resurrection power flowing out of His presence that they lived in communion with.

> As I stand by faith in Your Courts, Lord, I ask for the power of Your presence to manifest. Thank You, Lord, that You are always present. However, I desire Your glory and the closeness of Your Presence where Your resurrection power is known. I know You are close to those who are of a broken spirit and contrite heart. May I be that one who is yielded to You from the depths of my being. Come, Holy Spirit, and show Yourself glorious in Jesus' Name. Amen.

Abraham had a God who resurrected dead things. The third thing connected to Abraham and Sarah's resurrection was the way they saw the Lord. Notice again that Romans 4:17 declares that Abraham and Sarah's God was the one who *gives life to the dead.* This is resurrection and revival. They had a God displayed and revealed to them who could bring dead things back to life. Their own bodies were resurrected, which allowed them to conceive and give birth to Isaac. This belief in the power of God to resurrect also caused Abraham to pass the test when told to offer Isaac on an altar. Hebrews 11:17-19 attests to this reality.

> *By faith Abraham, when he was tested, offered up Isaac, and he who had received the promises offered*

up his only begotten son, of whom it was said, "In Isaac your seed shall be called," concluding that God was able to raise him up, even from the dead, from which he also received him in a figurative sense.

Notice that Abraham was convinced that even if Isaac died, God would raise him back up. He concluded this because of the word he had from the Lord previously, that "*In Isaac your seed shall be called*" Abraham was so persuaded of God's heart, power, and covenant keeping nature that he believed Isaac would be resurrected, even if offered and killed. This was born out of his confidence in a God who raises dead things back to life. His faith in God came from this revelation of who God really is.

The question is, is this our God as well? Even when things seem to have died and things might seem finalized, we serve a God who resurrects. This was the God of Abraham and Sarah. We should endeavor to have it recorded and stated in the Courts of Heaven that this is who we believe our God to be.

As we come into Your presence, Lord, in the Courts of Heaven, I ask that it might be recorded that I believe You are the God of resurrection. Let it be known that my faith declares You are the One who brings dead things back to life. May this statement speak on my behalf as I stand in Your Courts and petition You for my breakthrough. I declare before You that I believe there is nothing impossible with You. In Jesus' Name, amen.

The fourth thing that allowed Abraham and Sarah to experience resurrection was they knew God called things that do not exist into reality. The Lord can speak a word and divine order can originate. He can create that which is seen out of the unseen. This is what Hebrews 11:3 declares.

> *By faith we understand that the worlds were framed by the word of God, so that the things which are seen were not made of things which are visible.*

We should realize that in this verse the Bible doesn't say that God created something out of nothing. It says He created that which was *seen* from what was *unseen*. Real faith is discerning the unseen realm and proclaiming it into the seen dimension. This is why the prophetic is so important. When we discern what is in the unseen world through the prophetic, we can pull it into the seen dimension. This was the God Abraham and Sarah served. They understood that God had spoken something into reality in the unseen place. However, they needed to see it manifested in the seen. Remember that according to Hebrews 11:1, faith is possessing something in the unseen world before it manifests and is evident in the natural world.

Now faith is the substance of things hoped for, the evidence of things not seen.

This is what happened to Abraham when He believed what the Lord said to him. Therefore, Abraham knew that what God had said would manifest as he added his faith to the word of the Lord. He would see what was in the unseen world show up in the natural. This is why we are so encouraged by the word of the Lord to *add* our faith to the word we hear. Hebrews 4:2 tells us that because the people of God didn't embrace and add faith to the word, they forfeited the promises for their generations.

For indeed the gospel was preached to us as well as to them; but the word which they heard did not profit them, not being mixed with faith in those who heard it.

The declared word of God cannot by itself bring about the purposes of God. We must be a people of faith and add our belief to it. When we believe the Lord with persistence, we see what is in the spiritual / unseen world manifest and be revealed in this natural / seen realm. As we stand in the Courts of Heaven, we can petition the Courts until this becomes a reality.

Lord, as I come before Your Courts, let it be recorded that I believe Your word. I believe that which You have spoken and that You are the

God who calls unseen things into manifestation. I believe this and add my faith to You and Your power. May all that You have spoken manifest and be seen in my life. May we see the reality of Your promises come to pass. Even if things seem to be dead, may they rise and live again. I take You at Your word and stake my life and future on the word of the Lord that You have spoken to me. In Jesus' Name, amen.

CHAPTER 5

ATMOSPHERE
IS EVERYTHING

When we investigate the miraculous ministry of Jesus, there are three recorded places where He raised people from the dead. I am certain that there were many more who were brought from death back to life. However, we are only told about these three in the gospels. I base this on John 21:25. We are told that if everything Jesus did was recorded, there would not be enough books to hold that record.

> *And there are also many other things that Jesus did, which if they were written one by one, I suppose that even the world itself could not contain the books that would be written. Amen.*

This is an astounding testimony to the power and authority that Jesus walked in during His three and a half years of ministry. This is why I believe signs, wonders, and miracles should be the norm for today's church. Even in the early church, the miracles were so numerous that they were considered common. Acts 2:43 tells us that the manifestation of power was so regular through the apostles that there were *many* wonders and signs.

> *Then fear came upon every soul, and many wonders and signs were done through the apostles.*

The word *many* in this verse is *polus* in the Greek. It means "to be so much that it is common." We mustn't make the mistake of thinking that only what is recorded in the Bible is all that occurred. The truth is that miracles happened with such regularity that they were a common occurrence. This New Testament people was a people greatly associated with the supernatural move of God.

This scripture in Acts 2:43 has special meaning to me. A few years ago, we were in a very difficult place of life and ministry. We had been betrayed and had suffered much harm from those we had counted as friends. During this time, I had a very significant dream. In my dream I was sitting on an airplane in first class waiting to take off. The flight attendant stood and called my name. I got out of my seat and went to her to see what she wanted. She said to me, "You've been upgraded." When she said this, I thought, *Where am I going? I'm in first class.* However, I suddenly realized that the plane I was on was a double decker plane. There was a level above me that I didn't know existed. She then said to me, "You've be upgraded

from your *seat* in first class to a *suite* in the upper level."
She then said, "You are now in *suite* 243."

When she said the number *243*, in the dream the Holy
Spirit said to me, "*Acts 2:43.*" As I awoke the next morning,
I did what anyone would do. I went and got my Bible to
verify what Acts 2:43 said. As I read the words of this
verse, the Lord said, "*I am upgrading you in apostolic signs
and wonders.*" I am still pressing into the fullness of this
word. When the Lord gives us a word like this, we must
push into it with our faith until we see the completeness
of it. I believe this is a word connected to the resurrection
life of Jesus for these days of revival we are in. We will
see apostolic signs and wonders manifest. These kinds of
signs and wonders are those which cannot be denied. They
demand a decision from those who witness them. This is
what happened in Acts 3:1-10 when Peter and John saw
the lame man at the Gate Beautiful healed.

> *Now Peter and John went up together to the temple
> at the hour of prayer, the ninth hour. And a certain
> man lame from his mother's womb was carried,
> whom they laid daily at the gate of the temple which
> is called Beautiful, to ask alms from those who
> entered the temple; who, seeing Peter and John about
> to go into the temple, asked for alms. And fixing his
> eyes on him, with John, Peter said, "Look at us."
> So he gave them his attention, expecting to receive
> something from them. Then Peter said, "Silver and*

> gold I do not have, but what I do have I give you:
> In the name of Jesus Christ of Nazareth, rise up
> and walk." And he took him by the right hand and
> lifted him up, and immediately his feet and ankle
> bones received strength. So he, leaping up, stood and
> walked and entered the temple with them—walking,
> leaping, and praising God. And all the people saw
> him walking and praising God. Then they knew
> that it was he who sat begging alms at the Beautiful
> Gate of the temple; and they were filled with wonder
> and amazement at what had happened to him.

This miracle was so phenomenal that the religious leaders couldn't deny it. Acts 4:1-4 gives us some insight into what happened as a result of this miracle and the sermon preached from it.

> Now as they spoke to the people, the priests, the
> captain of the temple, and the Sadducees came upon
> them, being greatly disturbed that they taught the
> people and preached in Jesus the resurrection from
> the dead. And they laid hands on them, and put
> them in custody until the next day, for it was already
> evening. However, many of those who heard the
> word believed; and the number of the men came to
> be about five thousand.

The church experienced great growth. The last time we saw a number recorded in scripture about the size of the church it was 3,000 (see Acts 2:41). Now as a result of this miracle people came to the Lord and were added to the church. The apostolic miracle that was performed by Peter and John *demanded a decision!* The decision was people giving their lives to Jesus, because they could see the reality of Him being alive!

This apostolic miracle was one that couldn't be *denied.* So often the level of signs and wonders we have had can be explained away or discredited. However, there is coming a level of signs and wonders that will not be denied because they are apostolic in dimension. This is what happened with this miracle. As the religious leaders debated what they could and should do with Peter and John, they had to admit the level of miracle they had seen. Acts 4:13-23 shows us their dilemma.

> *Now when they saw the boldness of Peter and John, and perceived that they were uneducated and untrained men, they marveled. And they realized that they had been with Jesus. And seeing the man who had been healed standing with them, they could say nothing against it. But when they had commanded them to go aside out of the council, they conferred among themselves, saying, "What shall we do to these men? For, indeed, that a notable miracle has been done through them is evident to all who dwell in Jerusalem, and we cannot deny it. But so that it spreads no further among the people, let us*

severely threaten them, that from now on they speak to no man in this name."

So they called them and commanded them not to speak at all nor teach in the name of Jesus. But Peter and John answered and said to them, "Whether it is right in the sight of God to listen to you more than to God, you judge. For we cannot but speak the things which we have seen and heard." So when they had further threatened them, they let them go, finding no way of punishing them, because of the people, since they all glorified God for what had been done. For the man was over forty years old on whom this miracle of healing had been performed.

And being let go, they went to their own companions and reported all that the chief priests and elders had said to them.

The leaders called this miracle *a notable miracle.* This is what apostolic signs and wonders are. They are notable miracles that cannot be denied. This is the level of the miraculous that God will upgrade us into. We should petition the Court of Heaven for this upgrade.

As we come before Your judicial system, Lord, we present ourselves before this Court. We ask, Lord, for the promised upgrade into apostolic signs and wonders. We ask that there might be miracles that would demand a decision and that cannot be denied. We petition this Court for what is written in the books of heaven concerning us. May we be Your vessels to demonstrate the life of who You are. May we with Your early apostles preach and declare the resurrection of Jesus from the dead and then prove it through massive miracles that cause the supernatural again be a common thing in Your church, Your people of power. In Jesus' Name, amen.

As we look into the resurrection ministry of Jesus, again there are three occasions when scripture shows Him raising people from the dead. One is Jairus' daughter in Luke 8; others are the raising of the son of the widow of Nain in Luke 7 and the resurrection of Lazarus in John 11. In all of these, when Jesus raised people up from the dead we can see principles to experience our own resurrection of what might have died.

In this chapter, we will look at the raising of Jairus' daughter. This was a girl who was 12 years of age who died from a sickness. Jairus was the ruler of the synagogue, which would have made him a known person of influence. The account of this resurrection is found in Luke 8:41-42 and also Luke 8:49-56. The reason this story is interrupted for a few verses is because on the way to heal this girl before she died, the woman with the issue of blood touched Jesus with her need. Jesus stopped to minister to her, and this disruption allowed the girl to die. Let's read this account.

> *And behold, there came a man named Jairus, and he was a ruler of the synagogue. And he fell down at Jesus' feet and begged Him to come to his house, for he had an only daughter about twelve years of age, and she was dying.*
>
> *But as He went, the multitudes thronged Him.*

Can you imagine the desperation that was in this father? They have tried everything to get his only daughter healed. It has reached a critical point and the girl is on the edge go death. The father, whose is a well-respected Jewish leader, must now make a decision. Should he maintain his status as a leader of the Jewish religion who is against Jesus on most fronts, or does he go for help for his little girl whom he loves more than life itself? The decision is really no decision at all. He must go get Jesus. He is near, and he knows that if Jesus can just come a touch his little girl, she will be healed and spared of death.

As he reached Jesus, to his relief Jesus agreed to come. The problem was all these people slowing down the journey. Then this woman touched Jesus and virtue went from Him. She was healed. Jesus stopped to dialogue with her. I can only imagine the fear, turmoil, and anxiety in this father as he waited for Jesus to get finished with these people and come and heal *his* little girl. Then what he feared the most happened. A messenger from his house reached him.

While He was still speaking, someone came from the ruler of the synagogue's house, saying to him, "Your daughter is dead. Do not trouble the Teacher."

But when Jesus heard it, He answered him, saying, "Do not be afraid; only believe, and she will be made well." When He came into the house, He permitted no one to go in except Peter, James, and John, and the father and mother of the girl. Now all wept and mourned for her; but He said, "Do not weep; she is not dead, but sleeping." And they ridiculed Him, knowing that she was dead.

But He put them all outside, took her by the hand and called, saying, "Little girl, arise." Then her spirit returned, and she arose immediately. And He commanded that she be given something to eat. And her parents were astonished, but He charged them to tell no one what had happened.

As soon as Jesus heard the negative report, He spoke a word of hope, encouragement, and comfort. He admonished the man not to let fear take hold, but to keep believing. Jesus promised that if he would stay in faith and not allow the emotion of fear to rule, he would see the glory of God.

Many times, fear will try and take hold of us. It will come at unexpected times. Yet if we will listen in those times, the whisper of the Lord will quiet those fears. We will hear His voice say, *"Fear not, only believe."* At this point, we must decide who we will believe. Will we believe the fear that is screaming at us or will we believe the voice of the Master whispering to us? The choice will be ours. We must decide who we will believe in this moment. It can determine the outcome of the situation we are in.

As they continued the journey to this man's home, they found upon arrival mourners creating a wrong atmosphere for the resurrection. Jesus knew that the miraculous could be dependent on atmosphere. He therefore put out all the naysayers who would ridicule. The Scripture actually says that the mourners were *laughing Him to scorn*. When we *scorn* something we are saying it is worthless, stupid, despicable, and filled with contempt. These mourners were not there to give comfort. They were there to annihilate faith and stop the resurrection from happening.

Perhaps the *mourners* in our live are people, or maybe they are just the voices of our own intellect and logic. *They* are anything that would challenge our faith as we believe for resurrection of that which has died. We must deal with them as Jesus did. He put them out! He did not give room to them. Samuel, as a prophet of God, had to deal with his own *mourning*. Saul, the one he had anointed to be king, had forfeited the anointing through his own disappointment. Therefore God had rejected him. We find this in First Samuel 16:1. God had to motivate His prophet to come out of mourning and rise again in the anointing.

> *Now the Lord said to Samuel, "How long will you mourn for Saul, seeing I have rejected him from reigning over Israel? Fill your horn with oil, and go; I am sending you to Jesse the Bethlehemite. For I have provided Myself a king among his sons."*

The mourning was causing Samuel to not go about his God-ordained duties and what the Lord needed him to do. The Lord told him it was time to arise and release the anointing again. As we believe for resurrection, it is time for us to stop mourning and allowing the mourners in our life to annihilate faith! We must get up, fill our horn with oil, and go. This in essence was what Jesus was doing when He put the mourners out. He was declaring they would not be allowed to determine what happened or didn't happen. Jesus understood things they did not. The spirit that was on them to stop this resurrection was going to be humiliated and set in its place.

Jesus dealt aggressively with this thing and would not allow its operation. We too must, with spiritual aggression, put out all the mourners. They cannot be allowed to create the belief system, atmosphere, or any other thing that will stop us from believing. Jesus allowed only Peter, James, and John with the girl's father and mother to go into where the body lay. Jesus' perspective was that the girl was only asleep. He had simply come to awaken her.

Just an explanation here: I personally do not adhere to the teaching of *soul sleep*. I'm not an expert, but my understanding is that there is a thought propagated that when we die we go into a place of soul sleep much like what we experience when we sleep naturally now. It is the idea that we are in a place of semi-unconsciousness. The next thing we will know is when we are awakened at the ultimate resurrection. However, this does not line up with other scriptures. For instance, if this is the case of those who have died, why do we have the *cloud of witnesses* functioning presently in heaven? They should be *asleep* somewhere. They are not. They are in heaven granting testimony before the Lord through their words and intercession. Plus, we are told in Second Corinthians 5:6-8 that when we are absent from the body, we are present with the Lord.

> So we are always confident, knowing that while we
> are at home in the body we are absent from the Lord.
> For we walk by faith, not by sight. We are confident,
> yes, well pleased rather to be absent from the body
> and to be present with the Lord.

None of this would hint at the idea of soul sleep. When Jesus said He was going to wake her up because she was only sleeping, this was not what He meant. He was alluding to the fact that raising the dead was as simple an act as waking a person up from sleep. Sometimes we make the supernatural much more difficult than it really is. The anointing and authority that Jesus walked in while in the earth allowed Him to bring resurrection life. It wasn't hard or difficult. It was as easy as waking someone or something from sleep!

As stated previously, atmosphere is very important to the supernatural and Jesus' resurrection power flowing. This is why Jesus took control of the environment. He kicked out the mourners who were ridiculing and scorning. He took a select group into the room where the resurrection would occur. Even though these weren't perfect in their faith, they were willing to learn and believe. We must know that perfect faith is not necessary for us to see His resurrection power. Faith is not the absence of questions or even fear. It is a choice to not allow the questions and fear to dominate or determine actions. Sometimes faith is moving in agreement with the Lord and His word in the *midst* of our fear and questions. The whole issue is willingness to believe and choosing to obey. Jesus took this opportunity to *train* His disciples. They would later be used to raise the dead as well. What they witnessed and learned from these moments would be invaluable for them in times to come.

As they came into the room where the corpse of this little girl was, the Bible says that Jesus said, "*Little girl, arise.*" The word *arise* is the Greek word *egeiro*. It is the idea of *waking someone up.* It means "to collect ones senses." Jesus simply spoke the word in the atmosphere of faith and the little girl *woke up.* A whisper from Jesus can bring dead things back to life. When we hear His voice, that which is dead will live again. John 5:25 gives us this principle.

Most assuredly, I say to you, the hour is coming, and now is, when the dead will hear the voice of the Son of God; and those who hear will live.

Jesus spoke this about the ultimate resurrection of the dead at the end of the age. However, the principle is the same. Dead things come back to life when the voice of the Lord is heard. Hearing His voice washes away fear, doubt, unbelief, questions, and anything else that would hinder us. When we hear His voice, dreams come to life again. Relationships can be healed. Futures can be reset. His voice has the power to bring life to anything and everything that has previously died. When Jesus spoke to this little girl and told her to wake up, resurrection life flowed into her immediately. His voice brings life to what is dead.

Lord, as we come before Your Courts we ask You for dead things to live again. Lord, I take control of my atmosphere. I repent for allowing the "mourners" to determine my atmosphere. I extract and remove these from any and all places of influence. I declare before Your Courts that even in my imperfect faith, You Lord will bring to pass Your resurrection life. I ask for Your word to come into my heart. I ask that Your voice might cause what is dead in my life to live again. Lord, allow dreams, passions, vision, relationships, restoration, and any other thing to live again in Jesus' Name. May my faith speak before You as I believe the whisper of Your voice and not the screams of fear. Let it give testimony in Your Courts that all that is written in my book might come to pass in Jesus' Name, amen.

CHAPTER 6

TEARS THAT SPEAK

Another recorded resurrection that Jesus performed was the raising of a widow's son in a little town of Nain. Luke 7:11-17 gives us the account of this resurrection.

> *Now it happened, the day after, that He went into a city called Nain; and many of His disciples went with Him, and a large crowd. And when He came near the gate of the city, behold, a dead man was being carried out, the only son of his mother; and she was a widow. And a large crowd from the city was with her. When the Lord saw her, He had compassion on her and said to her, "Do not weep." Then He came and touched the open coffin, and those who carried him stood still. And He said, "Young man, I say to you, arise." So he who was dead sat up and began to speak. And He presented him to his mother.*
>
> *Then fear came upon all, and they glorified God, saying, "A great prophet has risen up among us";*

and, "God has visited His people." And this report about Him went throughout all Judea and all the surrounding region.

The first thing that stands out about this resurrection is where it happened. Nain was not a big or significant place. It was off the beaten path. In fact, Nain was *a small farming village in Jesus' time,* nestled up against Mount Moreh, which defined the east side of the Jezreel Valley. The town itself was off the beaten path. Access to it was limited to a single road. Many times we feel insignificant, forgotten, and not important at all. We wonder whether anyone knows we are alive are even exist. Yet Jesus went to this little town of Nain. Jesus deemed this place important enough to visit it with His presence and with His power. If you are struggling with insignificance and wonder if the Lord would pay attention to you, the answer is yes. Jesus answered this question by bothering to go to Nain. He showed up in this out-of-the-way place at just the right time.

I have found that the Lord is especially drawn to those who feel less than others. There is something about those who feel left out and isolated that Jesus loves to come to. This is His nature toward us. Those who are discarded by others, Jesus goes to retrieve. Those who are abandoned by others, Jesus chooses to be His. Those who are rejected by others, Jesus draws to Himself. My admonition would be to allow your brokenness to propel you to the Lord.

He will not cast you away. He actually prefers you over those who think themselves important. We see this in Luke 18:9-14.

> *Also He spoke this parable to some who trusted in themselves that they were righteous, and despised others: "Two men went up to the temple to pray, one a Pharisee and the other a tax collector. The Pharisee stood and prayed thus with himself, 'God, I thank You that I am not like other men—extortioners, unjust, adulterers, or even as this tax collector. I fast twice a week; I give tithes of all that I possess.' And the tax collector, standing afar off, would not so much as raise his eyes to heaven, but beat his breast, saying, 'God, be merciful to me a sinner!' I tell you, this man went down to his house justified rather than the other; for everyone who exalts himself will be humbled, and he who humbles himself will be exalted."*

The one who was justified before the Lord was the one who saw his need. He asked for mercy and redemption. The one who thought himself worthy of something was ignored by God. The Lord is drawn to the downtrodden and to those who even feel unworthy of His love. He loves to come to them and acknowledge them with His acceptance and care. This would explain why, when Jesus was entering the town and saw the funeral possession, He had compassion on the widow. Her tears moved Him. We should know that tears carry great weight in the Courts of Heaven. Job 16:19-21 shows that our tears are giving witness in the Courts of Heaven.

> *Surely even now my witness is in heaven, And my evidence is on high. My friends scorn me; My eyes pour out tears to God. Oh, that one might plead for a man with God, As a man pleads for his neighbor!*

Job is stating that the tears flowing from his eyes were a part of the witness and evidence that was being presented on high. Our tears carry great weight in the Courts of Heaven. Job was aware of this and spoke of it as he presented his case before the Lord. The end result was that he was justified and received double everything he lost. Job 42:10 shows that as Job prayed for his friends and the witness of everything else he had presented before the Lord, God rendered a verdict for him. He was given back all that was lost and much more. He was given punitive damages as well as restoration of all things.

> *And the Lord restored Job's losses when he prayed for his friends. Indeed the Lord gave Job twice as much as he had before.*

There are times when the Lord will grant us punitive damages for our pain and suffering. In other words, all that we went through, we are rewarded for. As we stay faithful to the Lord during times of testing, all our tears cried through that time will speak on our behalf. God will remember us and reward us accordingly. Isaiah 61:7 actually shows the Lord promising double for all that was lost and the shame that was endured.

> *Instead of your shame you shall have double honor, And instead of confusion they shall rejoice in their portion. Therefore in their land they shall possess double; Everlasting joy shall be theirs.*

These are punitive damages. Punitive damages are defined as "damages exceeding simple compensation and awarded to punish the defendant." When the Lord gives punitive damages, He is not only rewarding us for faithfulness in difficult places, He is punishing the devil! This is what the widow in Luke 18:1-3 asked for from the judge. She asked that there would be a decision rendered *against* her adversary.

> *Then He spoke a parable to them, that men always ought to pray and not lose heart, saying: "There was in a certain city a judge who did not fear God nor regard man. Now there was a widow in that city; and she came to him, saying, 'Get justice for me from my adversary.'"*

Notice that she requested and petitioned this court to make her adversary pay. She said, "*Get justice for me from my adversary.*" When we please the Lord and our tears speak, Jesus is moved to compassion for us. He can and will render a verdict on our behalf that allows not just restoration but punitive damages from the devil. The devil is forced to give up what he has stolen away plus much more. We should petition the Court of Heaven concerning this and ask that our tears might speak and verdicts be rendered for us and what we love.

As I come before Your Courts, Lord, I ask that You might be moved to compassion at my tears. May my faithfulness in difficult times speak before You. May my tears be "heard" in Your Courts. Would You bring restoration and resurrection to my life. Everything that has been lost, Lord, would You restore. Lord, I ask that all that the devil has stolen from me, he would now be required to return. I also ask for punitive damages to be rendered to me. Not only make him give back what he took from me, but make him pay at least double according to Your word. Force him, my Lord, to repay all that was taken and much more. May I find favor in Your Court as my tears speak and give evidence before You. In Jesus' Name, amen.

As we said earlier, as Jesus was entering this city He encountered a funeral procession. Jesus stopped the procession. This is a picture of Jesus' power to stop the *death process*. We know that before this is over, the dead man will be raised back to life. Many times there is a death process that is working in us. Sickness, disease, depression, hopelessness, despair, and other things are stealing our life away. We are told that the enemy is a thief in John 10:10.

The thief does not come except to steal, and to kill, and to destroy. I have come that they may have life, and that they may have it more abundantly.

As the *thief*, satan comes to steal, kill, and destroy. However, Jesus is the One who brings life and life with abundance. Stealing, killing, and destroying is the *death process*. Perhaps you feel like you are caught in the devil's *death process*. Jesus is the One who will bring you out of this place and back into His life. This is what He did for this man in the coffin. He stopped the *death process* and brought life back again.

The first thing Jesus did to stop this death process and bring resurrection was to speak to the woman from His compassion. He told her to *not to weep*. Jesus telling her *not to weep* was the first clue that a miracle of resurrection was about to happen. It also spoke to the fact that her tears had touched something in heaven and therefore the time of weeping was over. Remember in Revelation 5:4-5 where John was told not to weep anymore?

So I wept much, because no one was found worthy to open and read the scroll, or to look at it. But one of the elders said to me, "Do not weep. Behold, the Lion of the tribe of Judah, the Root of David, has prevailed to open the scroll and to loose its seven seals."

The tears of John were sufficient. I believe that his apostolic tears agreed with the sacrifice of Jesus as the Lamb and now the Lion of the tribe of Judah. It was sufficient for the books to be open so that what heaven desired might be accomplished. There is a need for tears of intercession. Once these tears are supplied under the groanings of the Spirit of God (which we will get to later) there is no more need for tears. When Jesus told the woman to weep no more, He was declaring the tears were sufficient. Heaven had heard and the evidence of her tears had touched the throne.

In fact, to weep after a certain point can be counterproductive. What can begin as a real realm of intercession can turn into just a place of deep sorrow and grief. This does no one any good. We are told in Ecclesiastes 3:1 and 4 that there is a time for everything.

To everything there is a season, A time for every purpose under heaven.

A time to weep, And a time to laugh; A time to mourn, And a time to dance.

We must recognize the time we are in. Otherwise, we get no benefit from our activity. Hebrews 6:1-3 tells us that there is a time to move on. If we stay stuck in a place of weeping too long, it will cause us to forfeit the true destiny of God. Weeping is a necessary aspect of Courtroom activity. However, once it is sufficient we must go forward.

Therefore, leaving the discussion of the elementary principles of Christ, let us go on to perfection, not laying again the foundation of repentance from dead works and of faith toward God, of the doctrine of baptisms, of laying on of hands, of resurrection of the dead, and of eternal judgment. And this we will do if God permits.

We are to *leave* something and move forward. One of the things we are to *leave* is repentance from dead works. This is a place of weeping. There is a time when our repentance is sufficient. We don't need to repent any more. If we stay in this place it will become counterproductive. We will be hindered from moving into the full destiny and purpose of God. Notice we are to leave the *discussion*. It is not that we abandon the truth of repentance. It is that we use it as a platform to propel us into the next thing God has for us. Otherwise, we get stuck in a perpetual place of repentance and weeping that will not allow us to move on. We will invariably develop an unhealthy perspective of who we are and not see ourselves as the righteousness of God in Christ Jesus. Jesus told this woman to *stop weeping*. Something marvelous and wonderful was about to happen.

The new thing that happens is Jesus touches the coffin and stops the procession. At this point the death process is brought to a halt. The significance of Jesus *touching* the coffin can't be missed. Anyone under Jewish law who touches anything related to death becomes unclean for seven days. Numbers 19:11 gives this dictate.

> *He who touches the dead body of anyone shall be unclean seven days.*

When Jesus touched this open coffin, this would have made Him unclean by Jewish law. However, Jesus was operating from a higher place. He wasn't afraid of death touching Him. He understood, as a New Testament man, that death didn't defile Him—He destroyed and defiled death! What was in Him was stronger and greater than death itself! If we are to operate in the power of resurrection, we must believe and know that *greater is He who is in me that he who is in the world.* We have the power to subdue death, not death subdue us. By touching this open coffin, Jesus was making this statement.

Please notice that as Jesus *touched* the open coffin, those who carried it stood still. Jesus' touch will stop the death process as we have said. However, once the death process is stopped, resurrection life still needs to flow. Jesus then spoke and awakened the young man. As with the young girl, He said to the young man, "*Arise.*" This is the same Greek word *egeiro*. Again, it means "to awaken and collect ones senses." We see that resurrection life flowing is an awakening that takes place. We wake up to a new *sense*. We become aware of that which we were not aware of before. This is the resurrection power of the Lord flowing in us. We begin to live life from a fresh place of revelation. This is resurrection life. Jesus has spoken and we have come to life.

We are told that this young man sat up and began to speak. The word *speak* in the Greek is *laleo*. It means "to talk, utter words, preach." This young man who had experienced the resurrection of Jesus began to preach revelation from his experience. He had seen the other realm, and I am sure he announced the glory of God. When we experience resurrection life, our message will change. It will be filled with the glory of God and His majesty and love.

Many years ago, I was privileged to be a part of a church where an emergency room doctor who was a believer had himself died. He had a heart attack suddenly, died, and went to heaven, where he saw glorious things. He was resuscitated and came back into his body. He was one of the gentlest men I have ever been around. He told of the love he experienced in that place called heaven. It changed him drastically, by his own account. He also said there were other things he saw that he was forbidden by heaven to tell. They were unspeakable. My point is, his message changed. He had encountered *Love* Himself. I am sure when this young man Jesus raised sat up and spoke, it was from his encounter. May we have such an encounter with His resurrection life that we too are changed for life in this earth.

The last thing we are told about this young man is Jesus *presented* him back to his mother alive. This mother must have had such great joy as the son she thought was gone was now presented back to her alive. Instead of going home alone, she now went home with her living son, all because they had encountered and intersected with Jesus at the city gate. His resurrection life had restored what seemed to be permanently lost.

Jesus desires to give back to us what might appear gone forever. He is the God of resurrection. Let's believe Him and appeal to the Courts of Heaven for this reality.

> As I come before Your Courts, Lord, thank You that such life flows from You that it overwhelms all forms of death. What might seem lost forever, You Lord are able to resurrect and restore. I thank You that You speak and Your voice causes what is dead to live again. Just as You raised the widow's son, so You say "arise" to what has died in my life and cause it to live. Just like the widow's future was not to live without her son, I thank You that my future is not to live without what is precious to me and from You. Let Your resurrection flow, I pray, as I petition this Court. May Your Name be glorified and may You be lifted up as

resurrection life flows in and through me. In Jesus' Name, amen.

CHAPTER 7

ROLL AWAY THE STONE

One of the most prominent resurrections of Jesus' ministry was the raising of Lazarus from the dead. It set the tone for Jesus' own death because of the impact of this resurrection. Lazarus had been dead and in the tomb for four days. The Jews believed that the spirit of one who died stayed in the earth realm for three days after death. They would have believed that, having been dead for four days, Lazarus' spirit would now have departed into eternity. On many levels, this made Lazarus' resurrection the greatest of Jesus' ministry. John 11:41-44 chronicles the actual raising of Lazarus from the dead.

Then they took away the stone from the place where the dead man was lying. And Jesus lifted up His eyes and said, "Father, I thank You that You have heard Me. And I know that You always hear Me, but because of the people who are standing by I said this, that they may believe that You sent Me." Now when He had said these things, He cried with a loud voice,

"Lazarus, come forth!" And he who had died came out bound hand and foot with graveclothes, and his face was wrapped with a cloth. Jesus said to them, "Loose him, and let him go."

The resurrection of Lazarus was so phenomenal that it was the last straw for the religious leaders and their agenda against Jesus. John 11:45-53 shows that they were convinced they could no longer allow Him to function. They were so afraid of His sway over the people that their only solution was to put Him to death.

Then many of the Jews who had come to Mary, and had seen the things Jesus did, believed in Him. But some of them went away to the Pharisees and told them the things Jesus did. Then the chief priests and the Pharisees gathered a council and said, "What shall we do? For this Man works many signs. If we let Him alone like this, everyone will believe in Him, and the Romans will come and take away both our place and nation."

And one of them, Caiaphas, being high priest that year, said to them, "You know nothing at all, nor do you consider that it is expedient for us that one man should die for the people, and not that the whole nation should perish." Now this he did not say on his own authority; but being high priest that year he prophesied that Jesus would die for the nation, and not for that nation only, but also that He would gather together in one the children of God who were scattered abroad.

Then, from that day on, they plotted to put Him to death.

The resurrection of Lazarus set in motion the final intent of the religious hierarchy to kill Jesus. As a side note, it is quite interesting that Caiaphas, who was high priest and yet a wicked man, *prophesied.* This is because the *position* he occupied had an anointing on it, whether he was godly or not. It is possible to function under the anointing and purpose of God even without His approval. This is a dangerous thing. It can convince a person they are *right with God* when things are not good. Perhaps this is the reason why the Lord said there would be those in the day of judgment who would not enter eternal life. Matthew 7:21-23 chronicles this idea.

Not everyone who says to Me, "Lord, Lord," shall enter the kingdom of heaven, but he who does the will of My Father in heaven. Many will say to Me in that day, "Lord, Lord, have we not prophesied in Your name, cast out demons in Your name, and done many wonders in Your name?" And then I will declare to them, "I never knew you; depart from Me, you who practice lawlessness!"

I do not question that these people actually functioned in signs, wonders, and the supernatural on some level. Perhaps God honored the position that they held. However, on a personal level they were not godly and practiced lawlessness. This applies to Caiaphas, who prophesied Jesus' death not as a godly man but as one occupying the position of high priest in his day. This all came about because of the resurrection of Lazarus. The divine purpose of God to propel Jesus to the cross was facilitated through Lazarus' resurrection. We are told in Acts 4:27-28 that it was the predetermined counsel of God for Jesus to die. The raising of Lazarus was a piece of the means God used to accomplish this.

For truly against Your holy Servant Jesus, whom You anointed, both Herod and Pontius Pilate, with the Gentiles and the people of Israel, were gathered together to do whatever Your hand and Your purpose determined before to be done.

The hand of the Lord determined before what was to be done with regard to Jesus dying for all people. The resurrection of Lazarus was a part of this plan. This is why, when Lazarus was sick, Jesus lingered until he died. Instead of going to heal him when the word came of his sickness, Jesus let him die instead, according to John 11:4-6.

*When Jesus heard that, He said, "This sickness is not
unto death, but for the glory of God, that the Son of
God may be glorified through it."*

*Now Jesus loved Martha and her sister and Lazarus.
So, when He heard that he was sick, He stayed two
more days in the place where He was.*

It's quite amazing the way Scripture phrases things
here. It states how much Jesus loved the family. Yet when
He heard that Lazarus was sick, He stayed two more days
where He was. Instead of rushing to heal Lazarus, He
waited. Sometimes we wonder *why* Jesus doesn't move for
us. *Why* the delay? It could be that a bigger thing is going
to be accomplished. When Jesus said the Son of God
would be glorified *through* it, this wasn't just speaking of
the resurrection. Jesus being *glorified* spoke of His going to
the cross and His own ultimate resurrection. We know this
because of John 12:20-24. When Greeks came and wanted
to see Jesus, Jesus knew the time had come for the offering
of Himself for *all* humanity. He wasn't just sent to the Jews.
He was sent for the sins and the people of the world.

*Now there were certain Greeks among those who
came up to worship at the feast. Then they came
to Philip, who was from Bethsaida of Galilee, and
asked him, saying, "Sir, we wish to see Jesus."*

*Philip came and told Andrew, and in turn Andrew
and Philip told Jesus.*

> *But Jesus answered them, saying, "The hour has come that the Son of Man should be glorified. Most assuredly, I say to you, unless a grain of wheat falls into the ground and dies, it remains alone; but if it dies, it produces much grain."*

Clearly the statement of Jesus about being *glorified* was a reference to Him being lifted up on the cross. So when He said that Lazarus was sick, but this was that the Son of God might be glorified, He was speaking of His crucifixion. He knew this would be used to propel Him into the predetermined will and counsel of God. He simply *stayed out of the way* until what the Father had arranged was set in place.

How often have we gotten in the way of what God has arranged? Jesus could have been moved by human compassion and rushed to the side of Lazarus. This would have completely upended the will and intent of God. However, Jesus being sensitive to the Holy Spirit waited and lingered so that what needed to be set up could be done. This allowed the purpose of God to be played out. We must give the Lord the space and time to arrange things for His purposes to be done. We should repent for any place we might have disrupted the desire of God through our own human strategies, emotions, and interference.

Lord, as I come before Your Courts and into Your judicial system, I humble my heart before

You. I ask that I would be sensitive and allow Your desire to be played out, even when my own human emotions might desire something else. I repent for any and all interference with Your plan and passion. Cleanse me, Lord, from rushing in where I should linger and wait. I'm asking that I might live my life in agreement with Your intent rather than my own. May it be recorded in Your Courts that this is my passion. May this speak before You on my behalf, In Jesus' Name, amen.

When Jesus came to the tomb of Lazarus, there was a process that was walked through to bring resurrection about. We can glean from this process that we might see resurrection power flow in us and through us as well. The first thing Jesus did to raise Lazarus up was to move Martha from *hope to faith*. As Jesus was met by the grieving Martha, Lazarus' sister, she expressed a confidence that nothing is impossible for Jesus. John 11:21-24 shows Martha making a statement that would allude to the fact that even though Lazarus was dead, there was something Jesus could still do.

> *Now Martha said to Jesus, "Lord, if You had been here, my brother would not have died. But even now I know that whatever You ask of God, God will give You."*

Jesus said to her, "Your brother will rise again."

Martha said to Him, "I know that he will rise again in the resurrection at the last day."

This dialogue has always intrigued me. In one moment it would appear that Martha is expressing hope and confidence that even now Jesus can resurrect Lazarus. Yet in the next breath, when Jesus confirms that Lazarus will be raised, she is stating that it will only happen at the resurrection of the dead on the last day. She is clearly torn and in a deep struggle with her faith. This is so much like us. We want to believe, yet the logic and reality of the situation seems impossible. This is what Jesus is about to deal with in Martha. As the oldest sister, she is the matriarch and must come into agreement with Jesus for this miracle to occur. First, Martha must move from hope in the future to vital faith in the moment. Hope by its nature is a confidence in what God will do in the future. We all have this and it brings us great comfort. Faith, on the other hand, is confidence in what God will do in the present moment and our agreement with it. Let me show you a couple of scriptures. Romans 8:24-25 is a very good reference for the nature of hope.

For we were saved in this hope, but hope that is seen is not hope; for why does one still hope for what he sees? But if we hope for what we do not see, we eagerly wait for it with perseverance.

Notice that hope creates a perseverance as we wait on the fullness of the promise to manifest. This is awesome. We need hope. However, hope is not the dimension where miracles occur. Miracles occur through faith. Remember, hope is believing in that which will happen in the future. This is where Martha was. At best she was vacillating between hope and faith. One moment she was saying that she knows God would do for Jesus whatever He asks. This was faith. The next moment she was back in hope declaring that her brother would be raised on the last day, which is in the future. We must move from hope to faith. Hebrews 11:1 and 6 tells is that faith *is*.

> *Now faith is the substance of things hoped for, the evidence of things not seen.*
>
> *But without faith it is impossible to please Him, for he who comes to God must believe that He is, and that He is a rewarder of those who diligently seek Him.*

In both of these verses, faith is described as being present tense. Faith *is* the possession of what we are hoping for. This means that real faith actually springs from the realm of hope. This is why hope is necessary. We can never have real faith in the moment if we aren't filled with hope. Martha had this, at least. I've seen many people who have become hopeless. There is no way for them to operate in real faith for resurrection to come to their situation.

During my pastoral years, I counseled many married couples. It was something I did as a pastor. One couple came into my office with major problems. The husband had serious problems as a control freak. What I mean by this is that through emotional manipulation—which included angry outbursts, moodiness, guilt, and other means—he dominated his wife. This had been going on for years. Through the years they had tried to work through it, yet nothing ever changed.

This final time, they were sitting in my office. I was seeking to bring some counsel that would alter what seemed like the inevitable. I said everything I knew to say, then suggested that we pray. As I stood and laid my hands on them both, I'll never forget what I immediately prophetically felt and knew. As I laid my left hand on her and my right hand on him, I felt her hopelessness. She had not an ounce of confidence that anything was ever going to change. I could *feel* it flowing from her. I prayed everything I knew to pray to try and spark something in her soul that would ignite a passion in her for her husband. Nothing happened. They left my office and were shortly thereafter divorced. The hopelessness in her gave no room for any confidence for the future, much less a place for present faith to erupt. There was no way to move her to faith because there was no hope in her for it to spring from.

Faith *is* the substance of what we are hoping for. Out of our hope faith can result. Hebrews 11:6 declares that to come to God we must believe that He *is*. This doesn't just mean that He exists. It means that we have a present revelation of God. This allows us to come to Him. He *is* and He *is* the One who rewards a diligent search of Him. What motivates this is real present-tense faith. We have a revelation of God that births in us the willingness to take a risk and believe Him in the moment. This is what Jesus was endeavoring to do with Martha. She had to move from hope into real faith. To accomplish this, Jesus released a revelation of who He was to her. John 11:23-25 shows Jesus declaring to her who He presently was in this situation.

> *Jesus said to her, "Your brother will rise again."*
>
> *Martha said to Him, "I know that he will rise again in the resurrection at the last day."*
>
> *Jesus said to her, "I am the resurrection and the life. He who believes in Me, though he may die, he shall live.*

Notice that as Jesus is moving her from hope to faith, He reveals Himself not as one who performs resurrection but as the resurrection and the life! This revelation and awareness of who Jesus is births faith to agree with Him for resurrection to occur. We must have this revelation to see resurrection occur. It is the revelation of who He is that moves us from the hope realm to the realm of faith.

It moves us from just a confidence in Him for the future to a present-day confidence for the supernatural to occur.

Another very important aspect in this story for resurrection to occur is to know *groanings* are necessary to resurrection. John 11:33 shows Jesus groaning in the spirit realm as He is preparing to raise Lazarus from the dead.

> *Therefore, when Jesus saw her weeping, and the Jews who came with her weeping, He groaned in the spirit and was troubled.*

The groaning that Jesus went through was a travailing in the spirit. We see this connected to resurrection in Romans 8:19-23. We are told here that the Holy Spirit creates in us a travail and groaning that will result in the resurrection of our literal bodies from the grave. When Jesus comes back we will be raised and changed like unto His glorious body. The thing that preceded this is the groanings of God.

> *For the earnest expectation of the creation eagerly waits for the revealing of the sons of God. For the creation was subjected to futility, not willingly, but because of Him who subjected it in hope; because the creation itself also will be delivered from the bondage of corruption into the glorious liberty of the children of God. For we know that the whole creation groans and labors with birth pangs together until now. Not*

only that, but we also who have the firstfruits of the Spirit, even we ourselves groan within ourselves, eagerly waiting for the adoption, the redemption of our body.

Please note that it is our *groaning* through the empowerment of the Holy Spirit that partners with the *groaning* of creation that results in the resurrection and the liberation of creation from its bondage! This means that what God will do, even in the ultimate event of history, we have a part to play. We must *groan* into reality this resurrection from the dead. This is why we see Jesus groaning in His spirit and being troubled. He was feeling the travail necessary to see resurrection take place! I believe the closer we get to this main event of history, the more the groaning of the Holy Spirit will intensify in our lives. Any resurrection requires the groaning of the Holy Spirit through us. This is why Romans 8:26 tells us that the Spirit prays through us with these groanings.

> *Likewise the Spirit also helps in our weaknesses. For we do not know what we should pray for as we ought, but the Spirit Himself makes intercession for us with groanings which cannot be uttered.*

I have experienced this many times in my own prayer life. I have felt the groaning of God moving through me. I have become aware that groanings in the Spirit carry great weight and testimony in the Courts of Heaven. *The groaning in the Spirit will do things in the Court of Heaven that words never can!*

I have a friend who is a successful businessman. I have watched him go from nothing to being a multi-millionaire. He attributes this to the Lord and His principles he has practiced. One day I got a call from this man. He began to tell me that through a process of events he had lost $500,000. He told me he had lain awake at night worrying about this and wondering what he needed to do. He had to be accountable to the bank and was afraid they would call due notes and debts he had with them. He wasn't worried about the ability to pay, but knew this would end his business. He asked me why I thought this had happened. He asked me what legal right he had granted to the devil that would cause this to happen.

We dialoged over the phone for a while and came to the conclusion that though he had started out wanting to expand the rule of the kingdom of God, he had digressed until it became about him and his success. He felt strongly that this was the cause of his trouble. He asked if I would go with him into the Courts of Heaven. I began to pray and ask that we might be granted entrance into the Courts concerning this situation. I then suggested my friend pray.

As he began to pray, he got no more than a few words past his lips when he began to sob incredibly. I have never heard such cries in all my life. Deep wells of travail were opened in him and he allowed it to pour out. There were no words, just sobs, groans, and travail. This went on for maybe a couple of minutes with great intensity. As it began to subside, I simply said, "May this be received and accepted as testimony before You, O God." My friend told me he had *never* experienced anything like this before. I knew, because of previous experiences in the Courts of Heaven in situations like this, that something had happened.

We hung up from our phone call. In about three hours, he called me again. When I answered the call, he was ecstatic. He said that after our time in the Courts of Heaven, a lady had called him. She handled grant money that was given away free and required no need to pay it back. My friend had never applied for grant money or requested it on any level. She ask him would he be interested in receiving $250,000 with no obligation. He told her he would. The end result was within three hours of standing in the Courts of Heaven and groaning and travailing, half the man's loss was restored. He has since then been greatly blessed and continues to increase! His groaning produced in the Courts of Heaven what words could never have done. He experienced the resurrection power of Jesus in restoring to him all that had been lost.

We must give room to the groanings of God if we are going to see His resurrection power manifest. Not only will we gain from it now, but we will be a part of groaning with creation to see the coming of the Lord, the resulting resurrection of the dead, and the liberating of creation from any and all bondages.

> As I come before Your Courts, Lord, I ask that You might produce in me through the firstfruits of the Holy Spirit the groaning that will speak in Your Courts. May the travail of my soul be heard in heaven. May the groaning of the Spirit of the Lord through me say more than any words I might utter before Your Courts. I make room and give place to these groanings of the Lord. Come, Lord, and take over my heart that Your passions might flow through me. Hear me, O Lord, and let Your Holy Spirit create in me that which will speak in Your Courts and allow resurrection to occur. In Jesus' Name, amen.

As Jesus prepared to raise Lazarus from the dead, He commanded the stone covering the tomb of Lazarus to be removed. John 11:39-41 tells us of Jesus requiring the stone to be removed. It also again shows Martha vacillating in her faith.

> *Jesus said, "Take away the stone."*
>
> *Martha, the sister of him who was dead, said to Him, "Lord, by this time there is a stench, for he has been dead four days."*

> *Jesus said to her, "Did I not say to you that if you would believe you would see the glory of God?" Then they took away the stone from the place where the dead man was lying. And Jesus lifted up His eyes and said, "Father, I thank You that You have heard Me."*

This was the moment when Martha had to move into faith from hope. She had to allow the stone to be rolled away. In any attempt to move into resurrection, we will all face this moment. Just like Martha, we have to be willing to face the stench. The stench of ridicule. The stench of failure. The stench of shame. The risk of facing the stench is the price of resurrection. Our willingness to believe God that He might bring to us His resurrection power is a necessary part.

Mary and I were led of God to plant what became a successful church work in a city back in the early '90s. We led and stewarded this work for 15 years until 2006, when we handed it to one who had been our executive pastor for 13 years. This man and his wife were dear friends of ours as well as ministry associates. We had always works from an apostolic perspective with regard to the church and its working. When we transitioned the church to their pastoral care, it was understood and agreed that I would maintain apostolic leadership and oversight. Our friends and associates would pastor the church; however, we would be honored as the apostolic overseers of the work. This worked fine for about three years. However, this man began to allow and even sow lies about me. The result was that the heart of the people turned against me. I would go in to minister as the apostolic father and feel the hostility toward me. A big part of this was the man I had trusted had betrayed me and allowed lies to be told about me without interrupting them. He himself was also a source of some of these lies.

To say this was heartbreaking is an understatement. Through a series of events we released the work and just moved on with life. We were living in another city and being blessed in our life, family, and ministry. Then I had a dream. In this dream, the one who had done the damage to me came to me with a legal document. He said to me, "I want you to sign away your and your children's rights to this city." I woke from the dream realizing that what I thought was a closed chapter in my life, God was not finished with. I knew the Lord was saying, *"You still have apostolic rights in this city. They are for you and for your children after you. Don't give them away."* The Lord was asking me to believe Him for resurrection of this work that was no longer there.

I struggled for quite a while. One of the main problems was that the people in that area believed wrong and bad things about me. If I was to return to this place, I would have to face the ridicule and shame of their opinions concerning me. After much wrestling and struggling, we knew we were to return and made that move. As we came back into that area, I began to pray. As I was praying one morning the Lord said to me, "*I want you to start again the work that was destroyed. Don't be afraid to roll away the stone. If you will roll away the stone, I will cause resurrection life to flow.*" I knew the Lord was asking me to not be afraid of the stench of lies, wrong ideas, and concepts against me. He was telling me that if I would take this step, I would see His apostolic newness of life flow and restore this work for me and my children.

We have actually seen this happen. The work is now moving forward. We have a strong onsite local group as well as thousands of online people who are a part of this house. God is faithful to His word. However, I could have been unwilling for the stench that I was going to encounter to touch my life. This could have been a point where the price was too great. I knew, though, that what hung in the balance was the intent of God for this region. I also knew that it was a place of inheritance for me and my children. If we are willing to face the stench, we can see the glory of God manifest in resurrection!

Another thing that happened that allowed Lazarus to be resurrected was Jesus operating in "kingship and priesthood." As Jesus approached the tomb, everything that was necessary for resurrection to occur had been done. John 11:41-44 shows the glorious results. Lazarus was raised from the dead and restored to Martha and Mary. Their faith in operation with Jesus had allowed this resurrection to happen.

Then they took away the stone from the place where the dead man was lying. And Jesus lifted up His eyes and said, "Father, I thank You that You have heard Me. And I know that You always hear Me, but because of the people who are standing by I said this, that they may believe that You sent Me." Now when He had said these things, He cried with a loud voice, "Lazarus, come forth!" And he who had died came out bound hand and foot with graveclothes, and his face was wrapped with a cloth. Jesus said to them, "Loose him, and let him go."

Notice that Jesus spoke to the Father about His *previous* prayer regarding this. He said to the Father, "*I thank You that You **have heard** Me.*" This means that Jesus on His journey to this place had been dealing with spiritual realities. He had been in the Courts of Heaven, dealing with any legal claim the devil had used to put Lazarus in the tomb prematurely. He did this from His priesthood. Remember that we have been made kings and priests to our God according to Revelation 1:5-6.

And from Jesus Christ, the faithful witness, the firstborn from the dead, and the ruler over the kings of the earth.

To Him who loved us and washed us from our sins in His own blood, and has made us kings and priests to His God and Father, to Him be glory and dominion forever and ever. Amen.

The main job of a priest is to get legal things in place. Kings, from this established place, then make decrees. For instance, Aaron as high priest was charged with going behind the veil once a year to set things legally in place so Israel would not be judged for their sins. He would go behind the veil with the blood of the Passover lamb. As he administered this blood, the children of Israel's sins would be remitted for the year. Hebrews 9:7 lets us know that the high priest once a year would make atonement with the blood for himself and the people.

> *But into the second part the high priest went alone once a year, not without blood, which he offered for himself and for the people's sins committed in ignorance.*

What the priest did behind the veil granted the Lord the legal right to be merciful to the sins of the people. This kept the judgment of God off the people for a year, until it was done all over again the next year. This was a prophetic picture every year of what Jesus would do in perfection for us. Hebrews 9:11-14 declares that Jesus has once and for all entered the tabernacle in heaven to legally atone for our sins forever.

> *But Christ came as High Priest of the good things to come, with the greater and more perfect tabernacle not made with hands, that is, not of this creation. Not with the blood of goats and calves, but with His*

own blood He entered the Most Holy Place once for all, having obtained eternal redemption. For if the blood of bulls and goats and the ashes of a heifer, sprinkling the unclean, sanctifies for the purifying of the flesh, how much more shall the blood of Christ, who through the eternal Spirit offered Himself without spot to God, cleanse your conscience from dead works to serve the living God?

The function of Jesus as our sacrifice and our High Priest legally secures for us redemption, forgiveness, mercy, and grace forever. The Holy Spirit takes what Jesus has legally done and brings application of it into our lives. I am saying all this to make a point that the main job of the priest was to get legal things in place. This is what we do as *priests unto our God.* When Jesus was praying on the way to Lazarus' tomb, He was functioning as priest. He was dealing with every legal issue that had allowed satan to kill Lazarus before his time. This had to be done or Jesus could not raise him from the dead.

If we are to experience resurrection, we must deal with any legal issue that has allowed the devil to kill, steal, and destroy. Once these legal issues are set into order, we can then stand as kings and proclaim and decree life into every situation. This is exactly what Jesus did. As a result of His function as a priest, Jesus now stood at the mouth of Lazarus' tomb and proclaimed, *"Lazarus, come forth!"* The result was that resurrection power entered the dead, decaying corpse and Lazarus came back to life and out of the grave! So it will be in every situation of our life where something has ended and died before its time. We can proclaim life back into it because the legal claims of the devil to hold it in death are now broken.

Once Lazarus was out of the tomb, he was yet bound in the grave cloths they had wrapped him in for burial. Jesus commanded they *"Loose him and let him go."* Once resurrection has occurred, there can still be the need to remove all hindrances. This will allow what has been resurrected to move in full liberty and power. Depending on what is raised into life, this can involve organization, attitude adjustment, perspective change, or other issues. Life is present and flowing, but there needs to be a freedom to move in its fullness. The joy of this new resurrected life is found in coming to great freedom and expression.

Jesus is the resurrection and the life. He desires to bring back to life everything that has died. He manifested this power through the raising of Jairus' daughter, the widow of Nain's son, and bringing Lazarus out of the tomb. As we operate in the Court of Heaven, we can see legal things set in place so what has died in our life might live. Jesus is the One who brings dead things back to life. Let's petition His Court for this to be our reality!

Lord, as we come before Your Courts, we ask for Your resurrection life and power to flow in our lives and situations. We stand before You as priests and deal with any legal issue used by the devil to "kill" something prematurely. We ask that what might have "died" before its time would be allowed to live again! We repent for anything in our lives or bloodlines that would have allowed the devil the legal right to kill, steal, and destroy. We claim Colossians 2:14 as a legal verdict on our behalf. We say that every case, charge, or accusation against us is taken out of the way, having been nailed to Your cross. Lord, we ask that it have no more right to speak against us. We now, by faith, roll away the stone and declare, *"Live again! Let what is dead now come to life, in Jesus' Name."* We also ask, Lord, that all restriction against that which is now alive be removed. Even as the grave cloths were taken off Lazarus, let all hindrances be revoked. Thank You, Lord, that from Your Courts we can apply what You have done for us as priests before You. We also from this legal place make decrees as kings. Thank You so much for Your grace and mercy as new life now flows into my life and circumstances. In Jesus' Name, amen.

CHAPTER 8

CAN THESE
BONES LIVE?

Throughout Scripture, the Lord is portrayed as the God who raises from the dead. There is nothing more final, from a human perspective, as death. Yet the Lord allows it to be known that He is the God who raises dead things to life. This reality caused the apostle Paul to be willing to lay his life down and to suffer hardship for the gospel. He was so certain and confident of God's power to resurrect that even literal death was no threat. Second Corinthians 1:8-10 states Paul's confidence in the midst of hardship. This came from his unshakeable belief in the resurrection of the dead.

For we do not want you to be ignorant, brethren, of our trouble which came to us in Asia: that we were burdened beyond measure, above strength, so that we despaired even of life. Yes, we had the sentence of death in ourselves, that we should not trust in ourselves but in God who raises the dead, who

*delivered us from so great a death, and does deliver
us; in whom we trust that He will still deliver us.*

The strength to get through the trouble they were
enduring was they *trusted in the God who raises from the
dead.* In a very literal way, it would seem that their ability
to endure the testing they were going through came
from believing if they died, God would raise them again.
Therefore, they had the *sentence of death* in themselves.
This meant they could give themselves even to death with
the certainty that there was a resurrection from the dead.

Believing that God raises from the dead is no trivial
thing. It greatly affects how we presently live and the
perspective we approach life with. I have experienced this
on a small scale. I pastored and worked in the local church
for 22 years. Then the Lord separated me to traveling
ministry. For 13 years I traveled as much as 240 days out
of the year. This means I was gone from my family this
much. Before this increased to this level I had a dream
about it. I was actually in South Africa when I had this
dream.

In my dream I had been sentenced to die. I knew
because I was going to die that I was going to miss much of
my family's life and experiences. I would miss birthdays,
anniversaries, holidays, and so much more. I knew my
family would do these things without me because I was
going to be dead. In my dream as the time approached for
me to die, I began to help those designated to put me to

death with the electrodes that would be attached to my body to electrocute me to death. I was actually helping them place these on my body. My family one by one came to tell me goodbye. I remember feeling sadness, but I was aware this must be done.

One of the things that stood out the most to me was my family wasn't real sad that I was going to be dead. There was some sorrow, but not much. This was the whole dream. As I woke up, the Lord said to me, "*I want to use you to touch the nations. It will require you to take the 'sentence of death' into yourself. You must be willing to die. If you will do this, I will put a grace on you that will cause your sacrifice to not be a grievous thing. I will also put a grace on your family so this will not be a grievous thing to them.*"

This is exactly what happened. I traveled so much by myself and without my family. There was a definite grace on our lives. This was because I took the *sentence of death* into myself. This was what I was doing by helping with the death process in my dream. There was a grace associated with this that empowered me. We have since then experienced the resurrection of the Lord into our lives. The years of sacrifice that we made, I believe, speak in the Courts of Heaven for us. They cause God to remember us so that now in this time we are blessed with family time and great intimacy.

When we are willing to make sacrifices because we believe in the God who raises from the dead, He will reward with resurrection. I didn't make the sacrifice hoping to later have this family time. As far as I was concerned, this was my life. However, the Lord is gracious and kind and rewards abundantly for any and all sacrifices we might make.

> Lord, as I stand in Your Courts, would You allow it to be recorded that I believe in Your power to raise dead things to life. Therefore, I take to myself the sentence of death. I will obey You fully and pay the cost of anything associated with this obedience. May my obedience to Your ways speak in Your Courts for me. May I be one who is willing to lay down my life for Your desires. Let it be known that whatever is required for me to sacrifice, I will give it, believing You are the God who raises dead things to life. In Jesus' Name, amen.

Ezekiel, it would appear, was used by God to bring resurrection into a disassembled situation. He was set by God in a valley of dry bones and told to prophesy. This account is in Ezekiel 37:1-14:

> *The hand of the Lord came upon me and brought me out in the Spirit of the Lord, and set me down in the midst of the valley; and it was full of bones. Then He caused me to pass by them all around, and behold, there were very many in the open valley; and indeed*

they were very dry. And He said to me, "Son of man, can these bones live?"

So I answered, "O Lord God, You know."

Again He said to me, "Prophesy to these bones, and say to them, 'O dry bones, hear the word of the Lord! Thus says the Lord God to these bones: "Surely I will cause breath to enter into you, and you shall live. I will put sinews on you and bring flesh upon you, cover you with skin and put breath in you; and you shall live. Then you shall know that I am the Lord." ' "

So I prophesied as I was commanded; and as I prophesied, there was a noise, and suddenly a rattling; and the bones came together, bone to bone. Indeed, as I looked, the sinews and the flesh came upon them, and the skin covered them over; but there was no breath in them.

Also He said to me, "Prophesy to the breath, prophesy, son of man, and say to the breath, 'Thus says the Lord God: "Come from the four winds, O breath, and breathe on these slain, that they may live." ' " So I prophesied as He commanded me, and breath came into them, and they lived, and stood upon their feet, an exceedingly great army.

Then He said to me, "Son of man, these bones are the whole house of Israel. They indeed say, 'Our bones are dry, our hope is lost, and we ourselves are cut off!' Therefore prophesy and say to them, 'Thus says the

Lord God: "Behold, O My people, I will open your graves and cause you to come up from your graves, and bring you into the land of Israel. Then you shall know that I am the Lord, when I have opened your graves, O My people, and brought you up from your graves. I will put My Spirit in you, and you shall live, and I will place you in your own land. Then you shall know that I, the Lord, have spoken it and performed it," says the Lord.'"

Ezekiel walked through the process of seeing resurrection life flow in this encounter he was having. He was an integral part of this process. Without him this resurrection would not have occurred.

The first thing we see is that God put Ezekiel in this place of death, barrenness, and brokenness. The situation seemed hopeless. So much so that when God asked Ezekiel if he believed the dry, broken, and scattered bones could live, Ezekiel was noncommittal. His answer was, *"Lord, You know."* In other words, "God, it looks really hopeless and useless, but I'm not limiting You."

Maybe this is your situation. Perhaps not only has something died, it has been disassembled and scattered into what would seem a million pieces. This is where Ezekiel was. Yet the Lord was about to do a major resurrection. Ezekiel was going to play a major part in this. We will also play a major part in the resurrection that seems hopeless and beyond help. Maybe you have been *set down* in an environment or situation where anything short of the resurrection power of God is insufficient. It could be in your work place, your family situation, or a ministry circumstance. Everything looks dead, dry, and disconnected. The good news is that God is able to bring good things to pass. He is able to release resurrection power into your situation. Let's pray this prayer.

> As I stand in Your Courts, Lord, let it be known that this situation seems impossible, yet I believe in You—the God of resurrection. Even as Ezekiel declared, "Lord, You know," at the question of could this live again, so I say this. I acknowledge, Lord, that You are God. Let this be recorded before You. I proclaim You are God and can do whatever You desire. You are able to bring life from that which is dead, dry, and disconnected. Lord, allow Your divine power to flow. Show Yourself glorious as I stand and petition Your Courts. Let life come again to these dry bones. In Jesus' Name, amen.

As Ezekiel looked at the situation, the Lord then told him to prophesy. At this point, Ezekiel had to decide what he would prophesy. Would he speak what his eyes were seeing or what his ears were hearing? His eyes saw the wasted desolation in this valley. However, his ears heard the sound of a marching army. Which one would he agree with? Would he prophesy what his eyes saw, or what his ears heard? His prophetic decree would determine what did or did not happen.

This is what so many do not understand with regard to the Court of Heaven. What we prophesy can determine what occurs. When the twelve spies came back from the land of Canaan, ten of them brought a bad report. Numbers 13:27-33 shows us the report that the ten brought back.

> Then they told him, and said: "We went to the land where you sent us. It truly flows with milk and honey, and this is its fruit. Nevertheless the people who dwell in the land are strong; the cities are fortified and very large; moreover we saw the descendants of Anak there. The Amalekites dwell in the land of the South; the Hittites, the Jebusites, and the Amorites dwell in the mountains; and the Canaanites dwell by the sea and along the banks of the Jordan."
>
> Then Caleb quieted the people before Moses, and said, "Let us go up at once and take possession, for we are well able to overcome it."
>
> But the men who had gone up with him said, "We are not able to go up against the people, for they are stronger than we." And they gave the children of Israel a bad report of the land which they had spied out, saying, "The land through which we have gone as spies is a land that devours its inhabitants, and all

the people whom we saw in it are men of great stature. There we saw the giants (the descendants of Anak came from the giants); and we were like grasshoppers in our own sight, and so we were in their sight."

This evil report/prophecy of these ten caused the heart of the people to melt. It also had an even bigger effect. It spoke in the Courts of Heaven against the nation of Israel. On the basis of this prophetic assessment, God rendered a judgment. They would wander for forty years because of the report/prophecy of these ten. Numbers 14:32-35 gives us insight into the judgment of God on the basis of the evil report/prophecy.

But as for you, your carcasses shall fall in this wilderness. And your sons shall be shepherds in the wilderness forty years, and bear the brunt of your infidelity, until your carcasses are consumed in the wilderness. According to the number of the days in which you spied out the land, forty days, for each day you shall bear your guilt one year, namely forty years, and you shall know My rejection. I the Lord have spoken this. I will surely do so to all this evil congregation who are gathered together against Me. In this wilderness they shall be consumed, and there they shall die.

The judgment based on their prophetic word was a year for every day the spies were in the land. The ten spies determined the destiny of a nation for forty years. Their prophetic word spoke against them in the Courts of Heaven and God rendered a verdict against them. Prophetic words are testimonies in the Court of Heaven. We must be careful what we prophesy and what we agree with.

Ezekiel had to decide what he would prophesy. Would he agree with what his eyes saw, which was desolation, or would he agree with the sound of the marching army his ears heard? He decided to prophesy the sound rather than the sight! This spoke before the Lord in the Courts of Heaven. We too must decide what we will *prophesy*. This determines whether we see resurrection or not. If we are negative and prophesy from that heart, we will have no resurrection power. On the other hand, if we prophesy from a spirit of faith we will see the resurrecting hand of God in our situations. We determine through our prophetic release what will occur. Let me picture for us what this could mean.

> Lord, as I stand before Your Courts, I release right testimony before Your presence. I decree, declare, and prophesy:
>
> The favor of the Lord is over my life. God's love is upon me and His face shines on me. I have favor with men as well. His face shines on me and gives me grace and peace in every situation. Divine doors open to me and opportunities are

presented to me that lead to great influence and success.

The Lord has ordained health and wellbeing into my life. I am free from every sickness and disease. It is removed far from me. I live a long and blessed life free of maladies and the torments created by health issues. There is no sickness, disease, premature, or untimely death. I live to the fullness of my days filled with long and satisfying life.

I am prosperous and filled with abundance on every level. I accumulate wealth behind the restraining orders of God from the Courts of Heaven. The devil is not able to devour the wealth and abundance planned for me from the Lord. His rights are revoked and removed. I am free to accumulate wealth and become the blessed of the Lord financially.

My marriage is blessed of God. I declare that my spouse is bone of my bone and flesh of my flesh. We walk in communion and harmony with the Lord and with each other. Our marriage is filled with love and companionship. We satisfy each other deeply and with great fulfillment.

My children are blessed after me. They receive generational blessing from my life. They are prosperous and successful. They experience the favor of God and of man. Every limitation comes off of them. They serve the Lord with great fervor and diligence. They are the godly seed that the Lord has sought after.

These prophetic declarations can be made every day of our lives. Through them we are releasing and presenting testimony in the Courts of Heaven. This grants the Lord the right to render verdicts for us.

As Ezekiel began to prophesy, that which was dry, desolate, and dead started shaking. The word in the Hebrew for *shakings* means "an earthquake." Earthquakes don't normally shake things together. However, this shaking or earthquake caused the dry, separated bones to come together. As Ezekiel prophesied, what was scattered began to be pulled together. This was a picture the Lord was giving the prophet about the regathering of Israel together as a nation and to their land. However, it can also speak to us of relationships that have been destroyed. The resurrection life of Jesus does bring reconciliation. As His life is pronounced and decreed, the ministry and word of reconciliation can be released. Second Corinthians 5:18-19 tells us that part of the ministry of Jesus is to bring reconciliation.

Now all things are of God, who has reconciled us to Himself through Jesus Christ, and has given us the ministry of reconciliation, that is, that God was in

Christ reconciling the world to Himself, not imputing their trespasses to them, and has committed to us the word of reconciliation.

As a result of us being reconciled to God, we now have the power to bring reconciliation. The rejoining of people to God and to each other is a manifestation of the kingdom of God. Whether it is in families, churches, businesses, or other realms of relationship, God desires to heal these. Destroyed relationships can be resurrected to new life. This is what can be pictured as Ezekiel prophesied. What had been severed and separated came back together through the shakings.

Sometimes, shakings are necessary to bring people back to each other. God can use dramatic and traumatic circumstances to cause people to recognize their need for each other. Pressures of life can either drive us apart are pull us together. This can happen as we prophesy resurrected life into relationships. The shakings can also be simply a stirring of good emotions toward those we are to be joined with. This can be the result of prophesying that life would began to flow into these relationships.

As Ezekiel continued to prophesy, sinew, flesh, and skin began to cover the now joined bones. It is quite interesting that there needed to be a continuation of the prophetic for the job to be completed. The Lord was not doing this separate from Ezekiel. Ezekiel was greatly necessary to see the resurrected power of God reconstitute these bodies.

The bones could speak of the reconnecting of lives while the flesh and sinew could be that which holds things together. Without the skin and sinew, our bones would fall apart. However, the ligaments and other parts of our body cause the connections to be secure. Things are held in place.

As Ezekiel prophesied, all this happened. The bones were joined and all that maintained the body was set in place. However, the job was not finished. There were now reformed corpses, but no life or breath. The Lord then instructed Ezekiel to prophesy to the winds of heaven. He was to declare the breath of heaven to come from the four winds. As Ezekiel prophesied, the breath of God entered the now arranged corpses and life flowed. The once dismantled and scattered bones now stood on their feet as a mighty army.

Many times, things are perfectly ordered and set, yet there is no supernatural life. It looks good, but there is still death clinging in a situation. Through the prophetic release, the resurrected life of Jesus flows in. Relationships are restored. Wounds are healed. Love is given that has been held back. What was separated and seemingly destroyed is reconciled and restored. This is because the resurrection power of Jesus is flowing as a result of someone prophetically declaring it into place.

The truth is that without Ezekiel there would have been no resurrection. The nation of Israel would have stayed in their graves. The Lord placed Ezekiel in the midst of what was dead and destroyed to bring life into the circumstances. So it can be with us. Perhaps you are in one of these situations. You can bring His resurrection life into this chaotic, dead, and destructive situation. Psalm 84:5-6 tells us that there is a people who cause places of weeping to become pools of blessings.

> *Blessed is the man whose strength is in You, Whose heart is set on pilgrimage. As they pass through the Valley of Baca, They make it a spring; The rain also covers it with pools.*

The word *baca* means "weeping." We are being told that when people who are strengthened by the Lord pass through this place, they cause a transformation. The place that was full of tears of sorrow becomes as place of springs of joy. The presence of a people who carry the resurrection life of God transforms grief and pain into glory and purpose. This is the people we are to be. Ezekiel accomplished this through the prophetic release of the Lord. The result was places of great dismay became places of great delight. This can be our experience as well. May we declare the right testimony before the Courts of Heaven through our prophetic declarations. As we do, we can see that which is dead live again.

I thank You, Lord, for the access to Your Courts granted me by the blood of Jesus. With confidence I enter into this place. As I prophesy from Your resurrection power, may that which is dead come back to life. May the Valley of Baca become a pool and springs of blessings. Let every lost or stressed relationship be healed in Jesus' Name. I prophesy bone back to bone. I prophesy that which holds it together set into place. I declare any and all attempts of the devil to separate people now to be silenced in Jesus' Name. I prophesy that the winds and breath of God might bring life into that which was slain. Allow Your presence to cause life to flow. As I make these decrees and declarations, may they be received as testimony before Your Court. May this be evidence presented that allows You as Judge to render decisions of life into every situation. I petition this Court and ask that the spirit, ministry, and word of reconciliation might be set in motion that Your resurrection power might manifest. In Jesus' Name, amen.

CHAPTER 9

THE POWER OF ALIGNMENT

There are many principles attached to the power of resurrection. We have seen several in previous chapters. We have seen that atmosphere is important, faith is important, the compassion of the Lord is important, and several others. Ultimately because of the subject of this book, we are seeing how God as Judge, from the Courts of Heaven, renders decisions that allow resurrection life to flow. We desire to see the reality of His power manifested in and through our lives. This requires that we be able to present cases in these Courts. One of the greatest needs to do this is proper alignment that grants us proper positioning in the Courts of Heaven. In other words, having a *status* in the Courts of Heaven is immensely important. Hebrews 11:39 tells us that those who got things through faith did so because they had a good testimony in heaven.

> *And all these, having obtained a good testimony through faith, did not receive the promise.*

These listed in Hebrews 11, and others, have a good testimony before the Lord. They obtained this testimony through their willingness to operate in faith. They chose to believe in the unseen world as much or more than the seen realm. This is what faith is. Hebrews 11:1,3,7 shows us that faith is believing as much in what we *sense* as what we *see*.

> *Now faith is the substance of things hoped for, the evidence of things not seen.*

Notice the words *not seen*.

> *By faith we understand that the worlds were framed by the word of God, so that the things which are seen were not made of things which are visible.*

The things that we see came from what was invisible.

> *By faith Noah, being divinely warned of things not yet seen, moved with godly fear, prepared an ark for the saving of his household, by which he condemned the world and became heir of the righteousness which is according to faith.*

Noah believed God in regard to things *not seen*.

We could continue our journey through Hebrews 11, and we would see this idea repeated over and over. Faith is putting confidence in the unseen realm even more that in what we can see. The people spoken of in Hebrews 11 gave up their lives because they believed the unseen realm so much. Not all died naturally, but all adjusted their lives and lifestyles because of what they could perceive in the unseen world. This is what made them people we talk of today. The result was they obtained this good testimony. In other words, the heavenly realm esteems and responds to them and their activity.

The truth is we do not have to die to have this power before heaven and the heavenly Courts. As we give up our lives for the sake of the gospel, we are granted status in heaven. This is why we are told in Revelation 12:11 that we overcome cases against us brought by the accuser of the brothers.

And they overcame him by the blood of the Lamb and by the word of their testimony, and they did not love their lives to the death.

The ability to overcome is afforded us by the blood of the Lamb, the word of our testimony, and not loving our lives to the death. The blood of the Lamb silences cases brought against us. The word of our testimony presents cases for us. Not loving our lives to the death grants us authority and status before the Courts. The more we agree with and submit ourselves to God's will, the more authority we can function in, in the Courts of Heaven. I am saying all this to make the point that we should desire status that allows us to petition the Courts on the highest level. This is what the widow of Zarephath experienced. She obtained a status with heaven through the principle of alignment. This pulled her into a place of power with heaven when her son died. First Kings 17:13-24 gives us the account of this widow moving in faith at the word of the Lord. The natural realm said the food was gone and they would die. However, when the prophet of God spoke the word of the Lord, she believed. Her faith put her in alignment with God through the prophet she believed.

> And Elijah said to her, "Do not fear; go and do as you have said, but make me a small cake from it first, and bring it to me; and afterward make some for yourself and your son. For thus says the Lord God of Israel: 'The bin of flour shall not be used up, nor shall the jar of oil run dry, until the day the Lord sends rain on the earth.' "
>
> So she went away and did according to the word of Elijah; and she and he and her household ate for many days. The bin of flour was not used up, nor did the jar of oil run dry, according to the word of the Lord which He spoke by Elijah.
>
> Now it happened after these things that the son of the woman who owned the house became sick. And his sickness was so serious that there was no breath left in him. So she said to Elijah, "What have I to do

with you, O man of God? Have you come to me to bring my sin to remembrance, and to kill my son?"

And he said to her, "Give me your son." So he took him out of her arms and carried him to the upper room where he was staying, and laid him on his own bed. Then he cried out to the Lord and said, "O Lord my God, have You also brought tragedy on the widow with whom I lodge, by killing her son?" And he stretched himself out on the child three times, and cried out to the Lord and said, "O Lord my God, I pray, let this child's soul come back to him." Then the Lord heard the voice of Elijah; and the soul of the child came back to him, and he revived.

And Elijah took the child and brought him down from the upper room into the house, and gave him to his mother. And Elijah said, "See, your son lives!"

Then the woman said to Elijah, "Now by this I know that you are a man of God, and that the word of the Lord in your mouth is the truth."

What a tremendous story. After the woman and her household had received supernatural provision for the famine, her son died. Why and how could such a thing happen? The devil never stops. However, the good news is that the man of God was present because this woman had aligned with him through her obedience. When the prophet had exhorted and released the word of God— that if she would give him the first cake, the supply would never end during the duration of the famine—she obeyed. She had, in fact, seen this occur. Yet her son died. The good news is that her obedience in honoring the man of God sent to her from the Lord allowed her to be aligned with him. She had drawing rights from the anointing that resided with her.

The truth is, we never know when we might need His resurrection power. Life can be unpredictable. However, if we have believed and obeyed the Lord previously, we are prepared to draw from the life of God. If this woman had resisted the word of the Lord through the prophet and had made it through the famine somehow and her son had died, she would have no connection to petition the Lord through. She would have suffered the pain, sorrow, and result of her son dying. This was not the case. Her obedience to the prophet's word had set her up for the time when she would need his resurrection power. Her alignment with the prophet gave the prophet the right to petition the Court of Heaven and make a case on her behalf.

Before I show you some of the principles that the prophet used to petition the Courts, let me unveil the idea of alignment. Alignment is a legal activity in the spirit world. Alignment is almost always connected to where and how we sow our finances. When Abraham honored Melchizedek with his tithe, it allowed Melchizedek to impart a blessing. Hebrews 7:6-8 shows the result of Abraham honoring Melchizedek with his tithe.

But he whose genealogy is not derived from them received tithes from Abraham and blessed him who had the promises. Now beyond all contradiction the lesser is blessed by the better. Here mortal men receive tithes, but there he receives them, of whom it is witnessed that he lives.

Abraham's tithe made a connection with Melchizedek so that the blessing of God from him as high priest could be imparted. When we operate in the tithe, we are connecting ourselves to Jesus as our High Priest after the order of Melchizedek. Our tithe testifies on our behalf before the Courts of Heaven. It connects us to Jesus' present-day life and activity for us as intercessor. It is absolutely appropriate to petition Jesus' influence into our lives based on our obedience with the tithe! However, the principle goes even further. By revelation, Abraham knew who Melchizedek was in his day. He recognized the honor due to this man as the high priest of God. Abraham, as the patriarch chosen by God to birth a nation, honored this man with his offering. This activity, just like with the widow of Zarephath and her offering, created an alignment in the spirit world. The revelation that Abraham had of who this man was allowed him to honor him with his finances. The result was an alignment in the spirit that allowed a blessing to be imparted.

Many times, we are asking for impartation of blessing without creating alignment through honor. The honor so often is depicted through finances. When this is set in place, heaven recognizes and acknowledges this. This is what happened when the widow cried to the prophet at the death of her son. Her alignment with the prophet allowed him to stand in the Courts of Heaven on behalf of this widow. Let's use alignment as a means of having status in heaven for resurrection.

> Lord, I ask as I stand before Your Courts that I would lay my life down that I might have status before You. May I be a person of faith who believes as much or more in the unseen world as the seen realm. I repent for any and all unbelief. I'm sorry for putting my confidence in the natural rather than living my life from the supernatural. Let this revelation alter how I live. I ask that I might come into an alignment with the right people. May my alignment connect me to those who have status before You. May I therefore receive breakthrough from the status that they carry. Let me continue to grow in my place before You. Let me practice the principle of alignment that will cause my case to be heard before You. May resurrection life be my portion in every part of my life. I love You, Jesus, and may You be glorified in and through me. In Jesus' Name, amen.

The prophet was allowed by God, from the status he held, to make a case for her because of her alignment. First of all, the woman considered that her son died because of her sin. Let's not discount this. Many times premature death is a result of bloodline issues. The iniquity and covenants made with demon powers can grant them a legal right to devour. This was the intent of the devil against my wife, Mary. A few years ago when I was in a hotel traveling on a ministry assignment, I had a dream.

In my dream, Mary was standing before me and made this statement, "I am getting stronger and stronger." I knew she was speaking of her physical wellbeing. As she was making this statement, her aunt Mildred was standing behind her. Mildred had been dead for 20-plus years at the time of this dream. Mary wasn't aware of her, but I was "seeing" her. As Mary was making this statement, Mildred was standing with her arms folded. She was shaking her head in disagreement. I knew she was saying, "No, she is in fact getting weaker and weaker and will die prematurely." I knew this was a result of a scheme of the devil against the women in Mary's bloodline.

As I returned home, I told Mary about the dream. I reminded her that her mother had died at 58 years of age. Mary then told me that her grandmother had died in her 40s. Very clearly, the intent of the devil was to take Mary out before her time. The Lord was unveiling his devices so we wouldn't fall prey to them. We then had a session in the Court of Heaven and knew through prophetic input that a covenant with devils through freemasonry was a significant source. Mary's grandfather had been a mason. She repented, renounced, and ask for all covenants with the demons to be annulled. We then also knew that someone in her bloodline had made a covenant with death. We asked for this covenant to be annulled also. The result was the right of the Lord to render a judgment against anything seeking to remove Mary prematurely from her life and assignment. It would have otherwise been a legal right of the devil to use something in her generational history. This was frustrated through Mary's repentance and the blood of Jesus speaking for her in His Courts.

This is similar to what this woman declared. She had an awareness that the case against her from her bloodline was allowing her son to die prematurely. She asked the man of God to deal with this. The man of God did three things that I can see in this scripture. First Kings 17:19 says the prophet took the son to his room.

> And he said to her, "Give me your son." So he took him out of her arms and carried him to the upper room where he was staying, and laid him on his own bed.

The word *staying* is the Hebrew word *yashab*. It means "to sit down as a judge." The prophet took the boy into the judicial system of heaven where he operated as a judge. It is possible and even desirable for us to move into a place as a judge in the Courts of Heaven. We are told in Isaiah 43:26 that we function with God in this capacity.

> *Put Me in remembrance; Let us contend together;*
> *State your case, that you may be acquitted.*

The word *contend* is the Hebrew word *palal*. It means "to judge in prayer." Prayer is not just petitioning the Lord. It can also be operating as a judge in agreement with His judgments and the ultimate Judge. This is the place Elijah stepped into as he contended for the boy's resurrection.

From this place of authority, he began to petition the Lord. Elijah began to make a case for justice. He was asking the Lord if it was a righteous thing for this boy to die. He said to God, "Have You brought tragedy on this widow with whom I lodge by killing her son?" This question reminded the Lord that this widow had taken him in and honored who he was. He also reminded the Lord through this question that because of what this widow had done, it would seem wrong for the boy to be dead.

Knowing how to present a case in the Courts of Heaven through the leading of the Holy Spirit can be essential to seeing resurrection occur. This prophet appealed to the righteous nature of God through these petitions. The prophet then stretched himself on the body of the boy three times. Through this act, he functionally imparted the anointing of God, which is the resurrection life of

Jesus. When legal things have been set into place, then the anointing is free to bring great life. The scripture says that God *heard the voice* of Elijah. In other words, his case on behalf of the woman was heard before God. The result was resurrection life flowing into the woman's son.

Thank You, Lord, that I can take my seat before You as a judge. I ask that what You, Lord Jesus, have done for me would allow me to take this position and place. Even as Elijah sat down as a judge, I take my place. I ask that any place where something from my bloodline is speaking against me would now be silenced. I ask that Your blood speak on my behalf as I repent for myself and any history of sin. I also ask that my sowing of my finances might speak before You as the widow of Zarephath's did. May I be remembered before You in regard to this. Lord, would You let any injustice against me be revenged. Even as You regarded the widow and caused a reversal of fortunes to come, so render on my behalf, I pray. Lord, I ask that You would allow Your anointing to flow into my situation and bring resurrection life. May the anointing of God break every yoke. Let that which is dead that I love dearly now live again in Jesus' Name, amen.

CHAPTER 10

DREAMS
RESTORED

Elisha received from Elijah the double portion of the anointing he carried. Elisha is recorded to have done double the miracles of Elijah. There are at least two miracles of resurrection attributed to Elisha. One was the Shunammite woman's son. The other was a dead man who touched Elisha's bones after his own death. In these accounts we can see principles for bringing dead things back to life from the Court of Heaven. The Shunammite woman was barren, it seemed, and could not bear a son. However, through the word of the Lord she conceived and brought forth a son. This son then died. As with all other resurrections, the raising of this son was not just a sovereign act. It involved the faith and activity of a people or person. Second Kings 4:17-37 shares this story of resurrection. It is an account of dreams met, dreams destroyed, and dreams restored. This is what the resurrection power of the Lord does.

But the woman conceived, and bore a son when the appointed time had come, of which Elisha had told her.

And the child grew. Now it happened one day that he went out to his father, to the reapers. And he said to his father, "My head, my head!"

So he said to a servant, "Carry him to his mother." When he had taken him and brought him to his mother, he sat on her knees till noon, and then died. And she went up and laid him on the bed of the man of God, shut the door upon him, and went out. Then she called to her husband, and said, "Please send me one of the young men and one of the donkeys, that I may run to the man of God and come back."

So he said, "Why are you going to him today? It is neither the New Moon nor the Sabbath."

And she said, "It is well." Then she saddled a donkey, and said to her servant, "Drive, and go forward; do not slacken the pace for me unless I tell you." And so she departed, and went to the man of God at Mount Carmel.

So it was, when the man of God saw her afar off, that he said to his servant Gehazi, "Look, the Shunammite woman! Please run now to meet her, and say to her, 'Is it well with you? Is it well with your husband? Is it well with the child?'"

And she answered, "It is well." Now when she came to the man of God at the hill, she caught him by the feet, but Gehazi came near to push her away. But the man of God said, "Let her alone; for her soul is in deep distress, and the Lord has hidden it from me, and has not told me."

So she said, "Did I ask a son of my lord? Did I not say, 'Do not deceive me'?"

Then he said to Gehazi, "Get yourself ready, and take my staff in your hand, and be on your way. If you meet anyone, do not greet him; and if anyone greets you, do not answer him; but lay my staff on the face of the child."

And the mother of the child said, "As the Lord lives, and as your soul lives, I will not leave you." So he arose and followed her. Now Gehazi went on ahead of them, and laid the staff on the face of the child; but there was neither voice nor hearing. Therefore he went back to meet him, and told him, saying, "The child has not awakened."

When Elisha came into the house, there was the child, lying dead on his bed. He went in therefore, shut the door behind the two of them, and prayed to the Lord. And he went up and lay on the child, and put his mouth on his mouth, his eyes on his eyes, and his hands on his hands; and he stretched himself out on the child, and the flesh of the child became *warm. He returned and walked back and forth in the house, and again went up and stretched himself out on him; then the child sneezed seven times, and the child opened his eyes. And he called Gehazi and said, "Call this Shunammite woman." So he called her. And when she came in to him, he said, "Pick up your son." So she went in, fell at his feet, and bowed to the ground; then she picked up her son and went out.*

This boy was a promise from God that seemingly was taken away. So often people have had real promises taken from them. The Bible actually says we should contend that we would receive and walk out a full inheritance in Second John 8.

Look to yourselves, that we do not lose those things we worked for, but that we may receive a full reward.

We must not lose the things we have labored for in the Spirit. We must obtain them and hold on to them that we might have a full reward. It appears that the devil came to steal what this woman had waited on for years. She had supernaturally been given this child. Now he was stripped away. The devil wants to take away anything God has blessed us with. We must know how to contend and hold on to what is ours. This woman did this by crying for resurrection. She got what was hers given back to her. How did this occur? Remember that all things are naked and open before the Lord. Hebrews 4:13 tells us that all things are seen and known.

And there is no creature hidden from His sight, but all things are naked and open to the eyes of Him to whom we must give account.

Things that we don't think speak concerning us, do for us in the Courts of Heaven. The testimony of who we are is speaking concerning us before the Lord. This was true for this woman, so that when she needed resurrection she could obtain it. The testimony speaking for her allowed resurrection to occur. The account says of this woman that she was notable. Seccond Kings 4:8 speaks concerning this.

Now it happened one day that Elisha went to Shunem, where there was a notable woman, and she persuaded him to eat some food. So it was, as often as he passed by, he would turn in there to eat some food.

This verse speaks of this woman being notable, so it seems this is how heaven saw her. She may have been of reputation in the earth too, but her real reputation was in heaven. This lady was full of honor, integrity, and uprightness. She was notable. The King James Version says she was *great*.

And it fell on a day, that Elisha passed to Shunem, where was a great woman; and she constrained him

> *to eat bread. And so it was, that as oft as he passed*
> *by, he turned in thither to eat bread.*

I believe this means she was *great* before the Lord. This is how Scripture speaks of John the Baptist. Luke 1:14-15 prophetically speaks of John before his birth.

> *And you will have joy and gladness, and many will*
> *rejoice at his birth. For he will be great in the sight*
> *of the Lord, and shall drink neither wine nor strong*
> *drink. He will also be filled with the Holy Spirit,*
> *even from his mother's womb.*

When someone is great in the sight of the Lord, this means they are highly esteemed and regarded. Their consecration to the Lord is of great value to the Lord. This was so with John. He lived as one wholly given to the Lord in every way. This caused him to be great in the sight of the Lord. We must know that the way we conduct ourselves can grant us reputation before the Lord. This bolsters our effect and power in the Courts of Heaven. We can see some of this woman's *greatness* in her activities toward Elisha. First of all, she valued character above gifting. When she wanted her husband to consent to building a room on their house for Elisha to stay, her motivation was Elisha's holiness. Second Kings 4:9-10 shares with us that this woman saw Elisha as a holy man set apart unto God.

And she said to her husband, "Look now, I know that this is a holy man of God, who passes by us regularly. Please, let us make a small upper room on the wall; and let us put a bed for him there, and a table and a chair and a lampstand; so it will be, whenever he comes to us, he can turn in there."

The woman wasn't even trying to get something from the gift Elisha carried. She simply saw him as one consecrated to the Lord. People who are great before the Lord have this trait. It speaks for them in the Court of Heaven. Many people can have gifts. Few, it seems, walk in a holy manner before the Lord. This woman discerned and valued that Elisha was a holy man set apart to the Lord in his life. She honored this. This honor of his holiness caused her to sow into his life. Probably without even knowing it, she practiced Matthew 10:41.

He who receives a prophet in the name of a prophet shall receive a prophet's reward. And he who receives a righteous man in the name of a righteous man shall receive a righteous man's reward.

When this woman and her husband honored the prophet by building the room on the side of the house, they honored God. Holy men/women of God are His representatives. When they are honored, it is as if God Himself is being honored. This honor spoke in the Courts of Heaven for this woman. When they received, helped, and kindly treated Elisha, this was of great value before the Lord. It caused the heart of the prophet to be stirred. His heart was stirred because this was speaking for the woman in the Courts of Heaven. Second Kings 4:11-17 tells us how the prophet prophetically declared something into place. His prophetic word didn't inform, it initiated. This is what many don't understand about the prophetic. When holy prophets speak, their words set in motion things to occur. They don't just inform of what God is doing; they cause the doing of it.

> And it happened one day that he came there, and he turned in to the upper room and lay down there. Then he said to Gehazi his servant, "Call this Shunammite woman." When he had called her, she stood before him. And he said to him, "Say now to her, 'Look, you have been concerned for us with all this care. What can I do for you? Do you want me to speak on your behalf to the king or to the commander of the army?' "
>
> She answered, "I dwell among my own people."
>
> So he said, "What then is to be done for her?"
>
> And Gehazi answered, "Actually, she has no son, and her husband is old."
>
> So he said, "Call her." When he had called her, she stood in the doorway. Then he said, "About this time next year you shall embrace a son."

And she said, "No, my lord. Man of God, do not lie to your maidservant!"

But the woman conceived, and bore a son when the appointed time had come, of which Elisha had told her.

Notice that when Elisha asked her if she wanted a special favor from those in authority, she had no interest. She wasn't trying to be something great or get something special. Again, this shows the heart of this lady and what God was honoring. The prophet then prophesied that she would get pregnant and have a child. This was the deepest secret longing of her heart. She clearly had been disappointed many times. Perhaps she hadn't been able to conceive. Maybe she had conceived but had suffered miscarriage after miscarriage. Whatever her trouble was, it had made her not want to try again. The pain of disappointment was so great, she didn't want to go there again. Through the prophetic, however, her secret was uncovered. The Lord not only gave her a son, but He also healed the decades of despair and disappointment. We know this because, when the prophet declared it, her statement implied she couldn't endure one more heartbreak. However, she received the desire of her heart because she had *received and honored* the prophetic in this holy man of God. This all spoke on her behalf in the Courts of Heaven. It gave testimony for her before the Lord.

As I come before Your Courts, O Lord, I pray that my life might make me great before You. Forgive me, Lord, for the times I have walked in a way that would not allow this. Let the heart and spirit of this lady be in me. May I value holiness above gifting. May I be looking for ways to serve without a hidden agenda. May there be a heart in me of honor that heaven respects. May I receive the prophetic and honor the vessels You have chosen to carry it. I ask that this all might speak before You concerning me. Even as You broke the barrenness in this woman, would You allow Your prophetic word to announce the conception of that which is holy in me. Let it be brought forth to Your glory and honor. In Jesus' Name, amen.

We know this lady did have her child, but then he suddenly died. This is where the resurrection took place. As I stated previously, the resurrection of this child didn't just happen. This woman's aggressive faith contended for her reward to not be lost. The devil did come to take it away, but her fervent faith secured the resurrection of her dead son. She did certain things that spoke in the Courts of Heaven for her. As the child died on her lap, she took the boy and laid him on the bed of the prophet.

The reason the prophet's bed was there in his room was because they had *previously* built it for him. So often people wait until they need something before they *build* something. By then, it's usually too late. The reason the room and bed were there was because of the previous sacrifice that had been made. This was speaking for her and her dead son! We must do the things now we will need later. If we wait until we need them then it normally will not work. Have we given, prayed, developed, served, and done other things that are speaking for us right now as we contend for resurrection? If we have, they will speak in the Courts of Heaven for us. They can be brought before the Lord to testify on our behalf. This will give us audience before Him.

As the woman contended for her son's resurrection, she controlled her emotions and words. When her husband and even the servant of the prophet asked her if things were okay, she said, "It is well." The truth was, it wasn't well. Nothing could have been further from the actual reality. Her son, her desire, her promise, and her future had died. Yet when she was asked, she refused to give in to hysteria and *agree* with the situation. She was definitely speaking through faith when she made this statement.

Our words have great impact in the Courts of Heaven. This was the one of the first things the Lord taught me about the Courts. The devil takes our words and presents them against us and against His will in His Courts. My son was beset by depression for over two years, and a big part of the problem was what I had said about him to his mother. I had spoken critical and negative things. The

Lord clearly showed me that the devil was actually saying before the Lord against my son, "Even his own father says this about him." I had to repent and ask for those words to be annulled. The result was my son being resurrected from this pit of despair.

This woman intuitively knew this. She refused to give place to the devil through giving an evil report. When asked if things were okay, she simply said, "It is well." This testimony of her faith spoke in the Courts of Heaven and prepared things for resurrection.

> Lord, as I come to stand before Your Courts, I remind the Courts of my previous sacrifice. Let it be recorded before Your Courts that I have honored the prophetic and the gifting You have allowed me to encounter. Let my previous sacrifice toward them and Your work speak for me now. I also ask that any negative word speaking against what I desire to be resurrected would now be silenced. I repent for my part in speaking evil and critical words. Forgive me, Lord, and let it now be silenced. Allow any and all cases of the enemy—against the things I am contending to be raised to life—let them now be annulled. Let Your glorious power and presence brings life and power into that which is dead, in Jesus' Name, amen.

This woman continued on in her pursuit of the resurrection of that which the enemy had stolen. She was not going to let go of her reward from the Lord. She secured a driver and told him not to slacken the pace for her unless she told him to. This speaks of an aggressive faith. So many people have a religious view of faith. They consider faith to be a *quiet believing* when in reality it is an *aggressive pursuit!* This is why their faith never obtains what they desire. If we are to get from the Lord what we need and desire, we must go after it with aggression. We must have a spirit that says no cost is too big to pay. No price is too much. Any sacrifice necessary, we will give. This is the voice and reason of real faith.

As they reached the prophet, he recognized this woman from a distance. This woman had so endeared herself to this man of God that he knew her. Have we served and helped on a practical level to the point that we are known? This woman had a special place in the heart of this prophet. When Gehazi came to push her away because she was intruding, the prophet arose to defend her. What wouldn't be allowed from others was allowed from her. This woman then made a case before the prophet. She said to him, "Did I ask a child from you?" In other words, this wasn't my idea. I didn't initiate it. Then she said, "Didn't I tell you not to deceive me?" This is exactly what I was afraid of—that once again I would get my hopes built up then have the dream snatched away. She was bringing the prophet into the situation with her by reminding him.

This is a wise woman. She knows that what God might not do for her, He will do for His prophet. Her honor and revelation of who Elisha is before the Lord is speaking for her. Elisha then sends Gehazi ahead with the staff to try and bring the boy back to life. However, the woman knows that only the prophet's presence will do the job. She will not be swayed. Only Elisha going with her will suffice. When they arrive at the house the prophet alone goes into the room. He stretches his body over the boy and he becomes warm. Then he walks back and forth in the room and does it again. This time the boy sneezes seven times and wakes up. The prophet then calls the mother and tells her to pick up her son. Instead, the woman bows at the feet of the prophet *then* picks up her son and goes out.

By walking back and forth, Elisha was praying and seeking the Lord. He then released the anointing he carried into the body of this dead boy. The result was resurrection occurred. I want us to see one more thing that is significant. Once the boy was raised up from the dead, when the mother came in to be reunited, she didn't even go to the son first. The first thing she did was bow before the prophet. This was a twofold expression. It was worship of the Lord and an honor of the vessel God used. This demonstrates the deep heart of this woman. It also shows us *how* we pick up what has been resurrected. We pick up from the Lord what has been resurrected through *worship*. Worship and honor cause us to be able to grasp what the Lord is giving us. In the midst of the dream, promise, and hope being given back to this woman, her first statement of adoration was to God and the one He used. Through this activity, she picked up in the spirit world what God had graciously given back to her. May we not forget to worship as resurrection life brings our hopes back to us. May we honor and adore the Lord, but also honor the vessels used to accomplish His will in the earth.

Lord, as we come before Your Courts, thank You that we are esteemed before You. Lord, I ask that I might so serve Your ministers that I would even be known at a distance by them. May my heart be one of such honor and love that it brings me into esteem with them before You. I realize this has great power before You. I also ask, Lord, as the anointing of God brings resurrection life back to my dreams, promises, and hopes the enemy might have stolen, that I would worship and honor. Even as this woman bowed in worship and honor in the act of "picking up" her son, so I love, honor, and worship You. Let me grasp through worship that which Your resurrection life has brought back from the dead. I worship You and honor those God has set into my life. May it speak in Your Courts for me. In Jesus' Name, amen.

CHAPTER 11

BONES OF LIFE

As we examine the resurrections that are recorded in Elisha's ministry, there is one more—after Elisha died, a dead man touched his bones. This dead corpse came back to life as a result of the anointing still contained in the bones of Elisha. This is an intriguing story and one of my favorites in Scripture. Second Kings 13:20-21 tells the story of this happening.

> Then Elisha died, and they buried him. And the raiding bands from Moab invaded the land in the spring of the year. So it was, as they were burying a man, that suddenly they spied a band of raiders; and they put the man in the tomb of Elisha; and when the man was let down and touched the bones of Elisha, he revived and stood on his feet.

There was a funeral happening. Bands of men were raiding and taking away possessions and bringing havoc into life in Israel. As this funeral was occurring, the people attending the gathering saw these raiders who would surely attack and pillage them. They couldn't get the funeral done without placing themselves in peril. Therefore, in desperation they opened the tomb of Elisha and put the corpse in it for safe keeping. They probably intended to come back when it was secure and get the corpse in the right grave. The problem was, when the dead corpse touched the decaying bones of Elisha, the dead man came back to life! Wow!

Elisha is in the afterlife. He is nowhere around. His spirit has departed a long time ago. So what allowed the resurrection of the man? There was no faith involved from anyone. Elisha isn't releasing faith. The man being buried isn't releasing faith. The people who are burying him are simply getting things done to try to get to safety. What allows this resurrection to occur? It is the *substance of the anointing* still in the bones of Elisha. The anointing of the Spirit is an essential part of the resurrection power of the Lord. As important as the legal aspect of resurrection is, we also must have the anointing of God.

We see this clearly in Luke 13:12-13. There was a woman bent over in a condition for 18 years. She had no ability to stand straight. When Jesus saw her, He had compassion on her. He then spoke to her and released the anointing.

But when Jesus saw her, He called her to Him and said to her, "Woman, you are loosed from your infirmity."

And He laid His hands on her, and immediately she
was made straight, and glorified God.

The word *loosed* is the Greek word *apoluo*. It means "to free fully, to pardon, to divorce." This word has to do with legal activity. Jesus legally set her free. The legal claims the devil had been using to hold her in this condition for 18 years were now revoked and removed. At this stage however, she was still bent over. It was only when Jesus *touched* her with His hands and imparted the anointing that she straightened up.

If we are to see resurrection life flow into different areas of our life, we must have the anointing of God. This means we should learn how the anointing works. In the occasion with Elisha and the man simply touching his decaying bones, the anointing resident in the bones brought the dead man to life again. One of my definitions for the anointing is the resurrection power of God. When the anointing of the Holy Spirit touches a person, what is dead in them can live again. The anointing has the power to drive away demons, restore diseased tissue, heal emotions, remove hindrances, and so much more. Isaiah 10:27 tells us that the anointing oil will destroy yokes.

It shall come to pass in that day That his burden
will be taken away from your shoulder, And his
yoke from your neck, And the yoke will be destroyed
because of the anointing oil.

Notice that the anointing of the Lord on our lives will remove burdens and destroy yokes. A burden is a pressure or weight that is on our lives. It is something that we worry about. It is something that dominates our thinking. A yoke is a limitation and controlling element. It tells us what we can do and where we can go. A yoke was used to control large animals and deny them freedom. The anointing oil will remove the burden and destroy the yoke! Once legal things are in place, resurrection life and power are demonstrated through the anointing. This is what happened to the woman who was bent. The legal issues were resolved at the word of Jesus and the touch of Jesus then released the anointing. The result of these two working together was freedom and liberty for the woman that she had not had in 18 years.

Elisha had received the mantle of Elijah when he was taken to heaven. You will remember that Elisha had served, fellowshipped and walked with Elijah for an extended time. When it came time for Elijah to be taken to heaven, Elisha asked him for a double portion. He was told that if he *saw* him taken away his request would be granted. We know this happened. Second Kings 2:10-14 chronicles this story.

So he said, "You have asked a hard thing. Nevertheless, if you see me when I am taken from you, it shall be so for you; but if not, it shall not be so." Then it happened, as they continued on and talked, that suddenly a chariot of fire appeared with horses of fire, and separated the two of them; and Elijah went up by a whirlwind into heaven.

And Elisha saw it, and he cried out, "My father, my father, the chariot of Israel and its horsemen!" So he saw him no more. And he took hold of his own clothes and tore them into two pieces. He also took up the mantle of Elijah that had fallen from him, and went back and stood by the bank of the Jordan. Then he took the mantle of Elijah that had fallen from him, and struck the water, and said, "Where is the Lord God of Elijah?" And when he also had struck the water, it was divided this way and that; and Elisha crossed over.

The key to Elisha getting the double portion of the anointing was to *see*. Walking in the anointing is about *revelation*. Whatever I see or have revelation concerning will allow me to function in the anointing and resurrection life of Jesus. Anointing accompanies revelation. When we see with our spiritual eyes, it unlocks the anointing of the Lord in us and to us. Elisha saw Elijah go. This allowed him to receive the mantle and walk in it. The result was he carried an anointing of great power. This anointing saturated his entire life and being. The anointing was clearly in the mantle that he picked up. However, his perpetual wearing of the mantle allowed the anointing to saturate his life all the way through to his bones. The result was the bones still carried the substance of the anointing even after his spirit had left his body.

This is quite often a little known fact concerning the anointing. This one reality concerning the anointing changed my life. I use to think mystically about the anointing. However, when I discovered that the anointing was an unseen substance that I could carry, I began to pray for people with much greater effectiveness. No longer was I crying to a God in heaven above. Now I was releasing the greater One who lives in me. This is what Peter meant when the lame man at the Gate Beautiful was healed in Acts 3:6-8. A beggar who had never walked experienced the power of God because of what was in Peter. Peter gave him the substance of the anointing that resided in him.

> Then Peter said, "Silver and gold I do not have, but what I do have I give you: In the name of Jesus Christ of Nazareth, rise up and walk." And he took him by the right hand and lifted him up, and immediately his feet and ankle bones received strength. So he, leaping up, stood and walked and entered the temple with them—walking, leaping, and praising God.

Peter gave him what he had. It was an impartation of the substance of the anointing. This is why the woman with the issue of blood was healed without Jesus doing anything. The anointing in Jesus' garment was enough to heal this diseased woman. She understood that the anointing resident on and in Jesus had saturated this garment. Matthew 9:20-21 tells us that the woman didn't even want an audience with Jesus. She just wanted to touch the garment. The result was her blood issue of 12 years dried up immediately.

> *And suddenly, a woman who had a flow of blood for twelve years came from behind and touched the hem of His garment. For she said to herself, "If only I may touch His garment, I shall be made well."*

Her faith reached out and attached herself to the anointing that was in Jesus' garment. She was instantly healed. This is why the handkerchiefs from Paul's body brought healing and deliverance in Acts 19:11-12.

> *Now God worked unusual miracles by the hands of Paul, so that even handkerchiefs or aprons were brought from his body to the sick, and the diseases left them and the evil spirits went out of them.*

Some believe that these were sweat rags that Paul used to wipe his brow as he labored to make tents. They carried not just the sweat of the man of God, but also the anointing that had saturated his life. The anointing, because it is a substance, though unseen can be transmitted and imparted. When we understand this, we realize the resurrection life of God is living in us. We stop just asking the Lord to manifest Himself and start manifesting Him instead. Greater is He that is in us! He is in us through the anointing of the Lord.

The truth is that we can legally deal with issues and still not see the results we desire. We can go before the Courts of Heaven and get legal things in place. Any resistance against us can be removed. This can all be done correctly and in order and we still do not see resurrection life manifest. The reason is we are not carrying a weight of the anointing that will allow this. There are varying levels of the anointing that can be on a person's life. We know this because Jesus walked in the anointing without measure according to John 3:34.

For He whom God has sent speaks the words of God,
for God does not give the Spirit by measure.

The reason Jesus performed such miracles of power was because He had an unrestricted anointing. This means there are different levels of anointing we can have. If we don't have a sufficient anointing, we can get legal things in place and not see the works of God manifest. When Jesus *loosed* the woman, there was sufficient power in His touch to make her straight. Jesus had received from the Lord the Spirit without measure. In other words, there were no limits on the anointing He carried. We also know there are varying levels of the anointing because we are told to ask for more. In Luke 11:13 we are told the Father will give *more* of the Holy Spirit if we ask Him.

*If you then, being evil, know how to give good gifts
to your children, how much more will your heavenly
Father give the Holy Spirit to those who ask Him!*

We are told in Romans 8:23 that we have received only
the "firstfruits" of the Holy Spirit. This would mean there
is much more of Him that we will not receive in this life.
The firstfruits of the Spirit is so glorious, what must the
fullness of Him be?

God is a good Father who delights in giving good things
to us. It is His pleasure to endow us with greater realms of
the Spirit of God. If we will ask Him, the Lord will grant
us new realms of anointing. The result will be a sufficient
anointing to set into place the works of God. When any
legal matter is settled in the spirit world, then we will carry
an anointing that will allow glory to manifest.

None of us will carry the Spirit without measure as
Jesus did. His call, consecration, and commitment allowed
the Lord to trust Him with this level. We can carry great
dimensions of the resurrection life of God. Regardless
of how great the anointing on our life, we can see any
dead thing brought back to life. We can do this through
successive impartations of the anointing. Even Jesus did
this. Remember in Mark 8:23-25 when Jesus healed the
blind man? It took two touches from the Lord to bring
complete healing to him.

So He took the blind man by the hand and led him out of the town. And when He had spit on his eyes and put His hands on him, He asked him if he saw anything.

And he looked up and said, "I see men like trees, walking."

Then He put His hands on his eyes again and made him look up. And he was restored and saw everyone clearly.

When we understand that the anointing is a substance that is resident in us, then we know what Jesus is doing here. The first touch of the anointing was sufficient to bring total healing. Jesus therefore took the substance that was in Him and *added* to what He had already imparted. This allowed total healing to come. If we can understand this, then we can impart healing and resurrection life to anyone. If the first time doesn't get the job done, then do it again. If that doesn't get it done, then add to it. Keep releasing the anointing until there is a sufficient release of this anointing to accomplish the task. The result will be the resurrection life of Jesus producing results that bring liberty and breakthrough.

The devil understands the legal realms of the spirit world. He will uses cases against us to forbid the anointing we do carry from having an effect. Even though I didn't understand the judicial aspect of the spirit world then, I experienced this in Cuba. I look back now and can see what the devil was wanting to do. My son, who was a teenager at this time, and I had gone to Cuba on a trip with a few other people. We were to minister for about a week. We got to the first city on a Saturday evening and immediately went to bed to get rested for the Sunday activities. As is my custom, I arose early to pray and prepare for the services that day. As I finished praying, I needed to go to the room of one of the people who had come on this trip. I had to go outside and walk on a walkway to get to his room.

As I was traversing, something caught my eye. I turned to look and it was young lady completely nude bathing herself. She wanted me to look and was flaunting herself at me. When I realized what was happening I jerked my head away and quickened my pace to the room where I was going. I knew the devil wanted me to compromise myself. I now know this was so he could get a legal case against me to restrict the anointing from flowing in and through my life. He looks for legal rights to accomplish this. However, in that moment I passed the test. I had a commitment to holiness and no compromise in the flesh.

We then went to the meetings. This gathering was led by a man who was an esteemed leader in the Cuban church. He had been imprisoned by Castro at least three times for preaching the gospel. This was a seasoned man of God who had paid dearly for his faith. It came time for me to speak. As I spoke, the presence of the Lord suddenly came into the room. The weight of the anointing suddenly appeared. I didn't know it, but in a part of the room I couldn't see, they had brought in a person on a bed who had been bedridden for eight years. As the anointing of God invaded the room, there was a commotion in that part of the room. Suddenly, someone emerged. People were ecstatic. They explained to me what the condition of this person had been. The Lord had suddenly healed them and they had gotten out of bed for the first time in eight years. They were walking and moving. It was a glorious time. The leader who was leading the meeting then came forward to speak. He said with tears, "I repent. I did not believe. I thought this was just another American who had come here to take pictures. Now I see the anointing." As a result of this meeting, everywhere we went across that island the next week, people would gather. Some traveled long distances to get to where we were. Miracles happened, bodies were healed, deliverances occurred, and much power was seen. This all happened because I didn't compromise myself and give the devil a legal right to restrict the anointing. I'm convinced this would not have occurred if I had.

If we are to carry a sufficient anointing to see these kinds of things happen and even greater, we must live in a way that grants the devil no legal claims against us. He knows the anointing is the resurrection power of God. He desires to stop it any way he can. He will always be seeking to discover a legal claim against this power. If we will live holy and seek the face of the Lord, there will be none granted him. The substance of the anointing that was in Elisha's bones will also be with us. It will bring life to every dead thing it touches.

> Lord, as I stand before Your Courts, I thank You for Your blood that grants me access. I thank You that legal claims to stop Your desire are revoked. The blood of Jesus speaks for me and causes these legal things to be ordered. I ask, Lord, that in addition to every legal thing being set, there would be a sufficient anointing resident in my life. I ask for "more" of the Holy Spirit. Let me live in such a way that any legal claim to restrict the anointing might be revoked. Help me, Lord, to be consecrated, committed, and called to carry the anointing necessary for resurrection life to manifest. Let the substance of this anointing now be upon me. Would You allow it to grow and increase so that new realms of breakthrough might come. I yield my heart to You and ask this in Jesus' Name, amen.

Chapter 12

DISCERNING
THE LORD'S BODY

My suspicion would be that Peter raised many from the dead in his ministry. After all, he walked with Jesus and saw all that He had done while on earth. The only occasion in Scripture, however, where we see Peter releasing resurrection power to bring one literally dead back to life was with Dorcas, or Tabitha as she was also called. We see this happening in Acts 9:36-42. This was clearly a major miracle that occurred in this region of the earth.

> *At Joppa there was a certain disciple named Tabitha, which is translated Dorcas. This woman was full of good works and charitable deeds which she did. But it happened in those days that she became sick and died. When they had washed her, they laid her in an upper room. And since Lydda was near Joppa, and the disciples had heard that Peter was there, they sent two men to him, imploring him not to delay in coming*

to them. Then Peter arose and went with them. When he had come, they brought him to the upper room. And all the widows stood by him weeping, showing the tunics and garments which Dorcas had made while she was with them. But Peter put them all out, and knelt down and prayed. And turning to the body he said, "Tabitha, arise." And she opened her eyes, and when she saw Peter she sat up. Then he gave her his hand and lifted her up; and when he had called the saints and widows, he presented her alive. And it became known throughout all Joppa, and many believed on the Lord.

We are told that Tabitha/Dorcas was a disciple. She was a part of the church in Joppa. It appears that she suddenly became sick, and this sickness led to her death. The fact that they sent to get Peter because he was close reveals a principle of resurrection that is quite often overlooked. In the church in Joppa, there was no one with the authority or anointing to raise Tabitha from the dead. There must have been a sense that she had died prematurely. It must have been that through the sickness the devil had been able to remove her before her time. Perhaps some had tried to raise her after her death, but it hadn't worked. As they became aware that Peter was around six to nine miles from them in Lydda, they sent for him. Their sending for Peter was with the understanding of the anointing and authority he carried in God. They esteemed him and the gift he possessed. This is what the Bible in First Corinthians 11:27-30 calls *discerning the Lord's body*. In teaching on the Lord's Supper, the apostle Paul makes this statement.

> *Therefore whoever eats this bread or drinks this cup of the Lord in an unworthy manner will be guilty of the body and blood of the Lord. But let a man examine himself, and so let him eat of the bread and drink of the cup. For he who eats and drinks in an unworthy manner eats and drinks judgment to himself, not discerning the Lord's body. For this reason many are weak and sick among you, and many sleep.*

As a result of not *discerning the Lord's body*, people were suffering with things that they shouldn't. Some had even died prematurely as a result of not understanding this principle. Again, the apostle Paul is speaking this with regard to the ordinance of communion. We must know that in communion, we are celebrating and remembering the body that Jesus offered for us on the cross. Jesus clearly told us in Luke 22:19-20 that when we take the bread and the cup, we are acknowledging and receiving from what He did in His *literal* body. There are powerful truths in this for us as we discern the weightiness of His crucifixion. However, there is another *expression* of His body and it is the *many-membered* body. This is us the church. Paul tells us in First Corinthians 10:16-17 that when we partake of the Lord's Supper, we are partaking not just of His literal body, but of the many-membered one as well.

The cup of blessing which we bless, is it not the communion of the blood of Christ? The bread which we break, is it not the communion of the body of Christ? For we, though many, are one bread and one body; for we all partake of that one bread.

Not only are we to discern and value the Lord's literal body that hung on the cross, we are to discern and value His many-membered one as well. This means that our revelation of who people are in the Lord is essential. The truth is all that Jesus died for on the cross is administered through the body of Christ. Yes, we can directly receive from the Lord. However, more often than not what God does in us and for us happens through His body. It takes the many-membered body to administer the anointing of the Holy Spirit that functionally supplies us all that Jesus legally gave us.

Remember, the Holy Spirit is here to apply into our lives in reality all that Jesus legally obtained for us. He does this through the many-membered body. However, if we do not discern who people are, we can cut ourselves off from what they carry. Second Corinthians 5:16-17 tells us that we must know people after the Lord and not in the natural. If we know them only in who they seem to be naturally, we can remove ourselves from receiving of the dispensation they carry in God.

> *Therefore, from now on, we regard no one according to the flesh. Even though we have known Christ according to the flesh, yet now we know Him thus no longer. Therefore, if anyone is in Christ, he is a new creation; old things have passed away; behold, all things have become new.*

We are not to evaluate who someone is after the flesh. We all do this, but it is unwise. We are to evaluate and discern who people are after the Spirit. We are to know them as the new creation of God and not after the old of the flesh. People allow idiosyncrasies to keep them from the anointing. They judge people by their mannerisms, personalities, and ways of doing things. They consider that God could never be a part of something like that. Yet He is so often. Our judgment of them in our own hearts and minds cuts us off from receiving of the portion of the anointing God has given them to carry.

This is one of the reasons why people were weak, sick, and dying prematurely in the Corinthian church. They were not discerning and valuing the anointing God had given to people. They were separating themselves from the very ones who could have administered the resurrection life of God into their lives. This is *not* what the people of Joppa did. They weren't competitive or jealous. They weren't envious of someone who carried something they didn't have. They didn't think that if they went and got Peter, he would upstage them and get glory and credit. No, they recognized he carried something no one in their midst did! Therefore, they sent for him. In this situation, they discerned the Lord's body and recognized the anointing and authority Peter walked in. The result was Dorcas/Tabitha did not die prematurely. She was resurrected and brought back to life.

Many times we don't experience the resurrection power of Jesus because we are critical, competitive, and will not humble ourselves before others. We perhaps don't like who they are in the flesh; therefore, we do not avail ourselves of what they operate in.

I was in a ministry situation where I had taught on the power and glory of God in healing. When I finished, the presence of the Lord came very strongly. One of the leaders came to me and asked where I got that power from. They were discerning enough to recognize these things don't just happen. They are usually the result of a divine connection that imparted something. I hesitated to tell them because *who* I received it from is quite often criticized. I actually do see why people are critical and judgmental, yet I never let the personality quirks turn me off. The ministry I was so impacted by that allowed this level of impartation has been criticized for extravagance, aloofness, rudeness, and other issues. Yet even though I could see why people could feel this way and judge this ministry that way, I could also see the level of anointing they walked in. Therefore, I chose to lay aside any judgments and connect so that I might walk in that anointing. After all, I had no say in the things being criticized, and they were between God and this ministry. All I knew was the level of anointing was much stronger than I had seen on anyone else.

The result was a joining that allowed this impartation that I carry to this day. The healing power of God functions in our ministry on the level it does today because I was able to see through everything others criticized and attach to the anointing God had chosen to bestow. I believe that God bestows anointing on *strange* people sometimes, just to see if we can receive it from them. Are we able to discern the Lord's body and get things from imperfect vessels because we recognize the resurrection life flowing through them? Romans 14:4 is a scripture we would do well to abide by with regard to these things.

> *Who are you to judge another's servant? To his own master he stands or falls. Indeed, he will be made to stand, for God is able to make him stand.*

Who do I think I am to judge someone who is the servant of God He has chosen to anoint? Their standing or falling is between God and them. My job should be to evaluate who someone is in God that I might be able to receive from them. When I do, I am accessing the resurrection power of God through a vessel I might otherwise have negated.

Instead of being weak, sickly, and even dying prematurely, I will be strong, healthy, and live a long and satisfying life in God. May the Lord deliver us from critical, judgmental attitudes that we might appreciate who people are in the body of Christ. We might see some Dorcases raised to life if we do.

As I come before Your Courts, Lord, I realize that I may have cut myself off from Your resurrection life through not discerning Your body properly. I repent! Cleanse me and forgive me for every arrogant and haughty attitude that would have dismissed someone because of things I didn't like about them. I am so sorry. Any case the devil has against me because of this, I ask that it might be revoked and silenced. I ask that I might properly discern Your body, that I might receive from the anointing they carry. That all that You legally obtained for me by Your sacrifice would be administered to me through those You have anointed. Lord, I choose to be as those at Joppa. I release all competition, judgments, jealousy, and ignorance and receive from the vessels You have chosen. In Jesus' Name, amen.

There is one more thing I would point out about the resurrection of Dorcas through Peter's ministry. Notice that when he arrived, he put everyone out, even the well-meaning people. As we have stated previously, atmosphere is very important for resurrection power to flow. By removing everyone, Peter was taking hold of the atmosphere and setting the stage for resurrection. The main thing I want us to notice, however, is that Peter knelt down and prayed. I believe he was ascertaining whether it was God's intent to raise Dorcas. Was it the will of God for Dorcas to come back?

When we are contending for resurrection of something, we must do the same thing. We must make sure it is God's will to bring something back to life. Sometimes, God intended for something to die. This can be very painful for us. We must be willing to let it go. Otherwise, we keep trying to bring back to life what God purposely let die. We do this with relationships, ministries, businesses, and other things. There are times when the Lord was finished with something and needed us to move on. However, we become emotionally attached and struggle with letting go and going forward. I'm sure there was much grief surrounding the death of Dorcas. The natural desire was that they wanted her resurrected. The question was, did God? Peter wanted to make sure that it was God's desire for Dorcas to come back and not just the people. Thus, he knelt and prayed to discern the will of the Lord in this situation. Clearly, he was convinced that God's purpose was to resurrect her.

The other thing that Peter was doing in praying was to discern if there was still anything resisting the resurrection of her. Once he determined it was God's intent to raise her, if there was still something withstanding in the Courts it needed to be revoked and removed. I believe that Peter dealt with any and all of this before he raised her from the dead.

> As I stand in Your Courts, Lord, I repent for trying to raise anything that You let die. I am sorry for contending where I needed to surrender to Your will. I ask that any and every emotional connection to anything You are finished with would be removed. I allow You to posses my heart and change my desires. I want to let go of the old and move into the new. May this be recorded before Your Courts that I am surrendering all to You.

> Lord, I also say before You that if it is Your intent to resurrect this back to life, let any claim against me or it be revoked. I ask that the blood of Jesus might speak and silence any and all voices. Let every legal claim be renounced and allow only the voices of heaven to now speak for me and this which is to be raised. In Jesus' Name, amen.

Notice that Peter prayed and communed with God to discern the Lord's will, but when it was time to resurrect Dorcas, he didn't pray, he decreed. One of our problems in seeing resurrection life flow is we keep asking God to do it when we should be doing it! When we decide it is the heart of the Lord for something to be resurrected, quit asking the Lord to do it. Just like Peter said, "Tabitha arise!" so are we to proclaim resurrection life. From the authority and voice of Peter, resurrection power flowed and she opened her eyes and sat up.

This might seem like a small issue, but it isn't. The posture we take in prayer can determine if something happens or not. When we, like Peter, have prayed through a situation, dealt with legal issues in the Courts of Heaven, and discerned it is God's will to resurrect, we should then begin to decree. It is not time to keep asking God. It is time to decree a thing until it happens. This is what Job 22:27-30 let us know. We are not only to petition, we are to proclaim and announce.

> *You will make your prayer to Him, He will hear you, And you will pay your vows. You will also declare a thing, And it will be established for you; So light will shine on your ways. When they cast you down, and you say, "Exaltation will come!" Then He will save the humble person. He will even deliver one who is not innocent; Yes, he will be delivered by the purity of your hands.*

We are to pray to Him, pay our vows, or what we have promised the Lord. We are to declare a thing and see it brought into being. Notice that when one is cast down, our word of decree will cause exaltation to come. We will speak and the innocent will be saved because of our words! This is the power of decree. This is what Jesu told His disciples when He sent them out to operate in resurrection power. Matthew 10:7-8 shows Jesus' commissioning of these.

> And as you go, preach, saying, "The kingdom of heaven is at hand." Heal the sick, cleanse the lepers, raise the dead, cast out demons. Freely you have received, freely give.

We are told that *we* are to heal the sick. *We* are to cleanse lepers. *We* are to raise the dead. *We* are to cast out demons. He didn't tell them to ask God to do it. He said *they* were to do it! We are to take our position of authority and, from who and what lives in us, release supernatural resurrection power. Jesus said what we have freely been given, release to others and in other situations. The result will be the resurrection power of the Lord flowing to bring dead things back to life. They will live again because we have stepped into the authority granted us by the Lord. We will not ask; we will announce. We will not petition; we will proclaim. We will not request; we will require. Resurrection life will flow and all that is to live will live again.

As I come before Your Courts, I repent for not taking my place of authority before You,

Lord. I will proclaim, announce, and decree a thing and see it happen. I will set into place the judgments of God from Your Courts. This is what I am doing through my decrees. I am announcing Your will and intent into place until it manifests completely. Thank You, Lord, for teaching me how to function in this level of authority from Your Courts. I receive it and walk in it in Jesus' Name, amen.

CHAPTER 13

CATASTROPHIC
TO COMFORT

The apostle Paul is in Troas ministering to the church in a lengthy service. Paul clearly has much to say to this church since his plan is to leave in the morning for his next destination. As he ministers well into the night, one who is listening to Paul preach in the third story of the building falls from the window to his death. Acts 20:7-12 tells us this story.

> Now on the first day of the week, when the disciples came together to break bread, Paul, ready to depart the next day, spoke to them and continued his message until midnight. There were many lamps in the upper room where they were gathered together. And in a window sat a certain young man named Eutychus, who was sinking into a deep sleep. He was overcome by sleep; and as Paul continued speaking, he fell down from the third story and was taken up dead. But Paul went down, fell on him, and embracing

him said, "Do not trouble yourselves, for his life is in him." Now when he had come up, had broken bread and eaten, and talked a long while, even till daybreak, he departed. And they brought the young man in alive, and they were not a little comforted.

This young man named Eutychus just couldn't stay awake. Eutychus was a common name of a slave. Perhaps this was who he was. His name means "one well-fated, to be fortunate." Perhaps this young man was sitting in the window to get some cool air from the night. For whatever reason, this tragedy occurred. The church had gathered to hear this eminent apostle. They had broken bread, had communion, and celebrated the sacrifice of Jesus. I'm sure Paul was imparting spiritual truth to them to strengthen their faith. He had spoken for a long time when this young man simply fell asleep and in their midst fell from the third story to the ground.

He died. What a heartbreaking occurrence. What had been such a life-changing day drinking in the wisdom and impartation of this apostle seems to end tragically. We are told that as Paul raised him from the dead he told them "not to be troubled." This word *troubled* is the Greek word *thorubeo,* and it means "a tumult, disturb, make a noise, set in an uproar." In other words, things were chaotic and in a catastrophic state. People were in a condition of fear and complete upheaval. However, the apostle Paul was not just carrying a kingdom of word, but also of power.

We are told in First Corinthians 4:20 that the kingdom of God is not a philosophy, but a power.

For the kingdom of God is not in word but in power.

The sad fact is, much of western Christianity has relegated the gospel to one of reason, when it is to be one of resurrection power. Paul tells us in First Corinthians 2:4-5 that any word he spoke had to release the power of God. Otherwise people's faith would be in just words rather than a present-day experience of the power of God.

And my speech and my preaching were not with persuasive words of human wisdom, but in demonstration of the Spirit and of power, that your faith should not be in the wisdom of men but in the power of God.

The wisdom of men will never hold people in difficult times. Experience in the power of God, however, will hold us and propel us through those times. People must be equipped with the resurrection power of God and not just good teaching. In Joshua 24:31 we are told that succeeding generations failed to follow the Lord because they knew nothing of His power. It is only the power of God mixed with good doctrine that holds us sufficiently.

Israel served the Lord all the days of Joshua, and all the days of the elders who outlived Joshua, who had

> *known all the works of the Lord which He had done*
> *for Israel.*

We do not know what Paul taught on this night in Troas. However, we do know that he raised up a dead young man. This is what is remembered about that night. This is what the conversation was about the next day and for many days. No one probably knew what Paul's message had been. They did remember the resurrection power of Jesus flowing into this boy though.

Another thing this speaks to me about is that Paul didn't have to stop and *get ready* to raise this young man from the dead. Paul lived his life in a *ready* state. What I mean by this is that he walked in such a way with the Lord that whatever was needed in the moment, Paul was prepared to confront the challenge. In Second Timothy 4:2 we see Paul exhorting Timothy to always be ready.

> *Preach the word! Be ready in season and out of season.*
> *Convince, rebuke, exhort, with all longsuffering and*
> *teaching.*

We are to always be walking full of faith, rich in the word, and filled with the Spirit. We are to keep ourselves in a readied state. Whether we know something is needed ahead of time or it is thrust upon us, we are prepared in our spirit. This was clearly where Paul was. He was ready in season and out. When this young man fell to his death,

Paul could jump into action and change an otherwise dire circumstance. The result was that what would have been catastrophic became a time of great comfort.

> Lord, as we stand in Your Courts, I ask that I would live my life in readiness. Help me not to live a compromising life but one of consecration. Allow this to please speak before You and Your Courts. Let it be known that I am a person who is ready in season and out of season. That should there be a need of resurrection life, I carry it with me wherever I go. Use me, Lord, as Your vessel to touch lives, even in an instant, should it be necessary. In Jesus' Name, amen.

The result of this resurrection was *comfort*. This is the Greek word *parakaleo*. It means "to call near." In other words, this resurrection spoke volumes to those present. It testified that they were *called near*. It spoke to them that they were the chosen of the Lord and that His favor was on them. There is nothing like the confirming and affirming life of God. It erases and eradicates doubts, fears, and uncertainty from our life. It makes us bold and sure in our God. When this young man was raised back to life, not only were they comforted that they would not live life without him, but they were assured that God was with them. When you know God is with you, nothing can overwhelm you. It doesn't matter anymore who is against you. Romans 8:31-39 speaks to this assurance.

> *What then shall we say to these things? If God is for us, who can be against us? He who did not spare His own Son, but delivered Him up for us all, how shall He not with Him also freely give us all things? Who shall bring a charge against God's elect? It is God who justifies. Who is he who condemns? It is Christ who died, and furthermore is also risen, who is even at the right hand of God, who also makes intercession for us. Who shall separate us from the love of Christ? Shall tribulation, or distress, or persecution, or famine, or nakedness, or peril, or sword? As it is written:*
>
> *"For Your sake we are killed all day long;*
> *We are accounted as sheep for the slaughter."*
>
> *Yet in all these things we are more than conquerors through Him who loved us. For I am persuaded that neither death nor life, nor angels nor principalities nor powers, nor things present nor things to come, nor height nor depth, nor any other created thing, shall be able to separate us from the love of God which is in Christ Jesus our Lord.*

The idea is not that we won't have things and people against us. The idea is they are of no consequence when the Lord is for us. When we are aware of the love wherewith

He loves us, it makes us more than conquerors. Even though we are "killed" for His sake all day, every day, we believe in the resurrection power of Jesus. To be "killed" speaks of the trouble, emotional strain, and pressures we are under. However, because of His love we overcome! Any charge brought against us is dismissed and revoked because we are the chosen of our God.

When this young man was raised, it called these people near and placed a boldness deep in their hearts. This is what an experience in the resurrection power of Jesus does for us. When you know that death itself is subject to Him, nothing can intimidate you and hold you in fear. You will serve Him and give your life if necessary with a confidence of His resurrection power.

> Lord, I ask that it be recorded in Your Courts that I die daily because I believe in Your resurrection life. Therefore, would You allow this life to flow in me and through me to others. I am convinced that nothing can ultimately destroy me. You have power over all things, even death. No one is able to bring a charge against me because of Your blood that speaks for Me. You Yourself are praying and making intercession for me. Therefore, I am more than a conqueror. Your resurrection power causes me to always triumph and prevail. I am unstoppable and victorious in all things

because of Your resurrection life. I ask that this would be presented before Your Courts. As a result of this, may You show Yourself glorious on my behalf. In Jesus' Name, amen.

CHAPTER 14

HEAVENLY PASSION

There is an occasion of resurrection found in Acts 14:8-20. The story begins with Paul healing a man born crippled. The result is the people seek to worship Paul and Barnabas. They convince them not to do so; however, things shift and Paul ends up stoned by some of the people who previously were trying to worship him.

> And in Lystra a certain man without strength in his feet was sitting, a cripple from his mother's womb, who had never walked. This man heard Paul speaking. Paul, observing him intently and seeing that he had faith to be healed, said with a loud voice, "Stand up straight on your feet!" And he leaped and walked. Now when the people saw what Paul had done, they raised their voices, saying in the Lycaonian language, "The gods have come down to us in the likeness of men!" And Barnabas they called Zeus, and Paul, Hermes, because he was the chief speaker. Then the priest of Zeus, whose temple was

in front of their city, brought oxen and garlands to the gates, intending to sacrifice with the multitudes.

But when the apostles Barnabas and Paul heard this, they tore their clothes and ran in among the multitude, crying out and saying, "Men, why are you doing these things? We also are men with the same nature as you, and preach to you that you should turn from these useless things to the living God, who made the heaven, the earth, the sea, and all things that are in them, who in bygone generations allowed all nations to walk in their own ways. Nevertheless He did not leave Himself without witness, in that He did good, gave us rain from heaven and fruitful seasons, filling our hearts with food and gladness." And with these sayings they could scarcely restrain the multitudes from sacrificing to them.

Then Jews from Antioch and Iconium came there; and having persuaded the multitudes, they stoned Paul and dragged him out of the city, supposing him to be dead. However, when the disciples gathered around him, he rose up and went into the city. And the next day he departed with Barnabas to Derbe.

The multitudes seemed easily persuaded. At one moment they were worshiping Paul and Barnabas, or at least trying to. The next moment, through the influence of others, they were stoning Paul to death. Some question whether Paul was really dead or not. However, even if he wasn't dead, he would have been so injured he could not have gotten up and returned to the city. This would lead me to believe that he was truly stoned to death. The Bible says the disciples gathered around him in a circle. I'm sure they were praying. Regardless of what they were or were not doing, Paul rose up and went back into the city. He was resurrected.

Some believe this could have been the time he speaks of in Second Corinthians 12:1-4 when he was out of his body. He speaks rather vaguely in his effort to communicate what he experienced. He even insinuates that maybe it was someone else, yet strongly suggests it was actually him. He spoke of seeing things unlawful to talk about.

> *It is doubtless not profitable for me to boast. I will come to visions and revelations of the Lord: I know a man in Christ who fourteen years ago—whether in the body I do not know, or whether out of the body I do not know, God knows—such a one was caught up to the third heaven. And I know such a man— whether in the body or out of the body I do not know, God knows— how he was caught up into Paradise and heard inexpressible words, which it is not lawful for a man to utter.*

In an effort to not try and impress people with this encounter, he seeks to deflect any glory. He doesn't want people thinking of him above measure. However, he says that he was caught up into the third heaven or the throne of God. He declares that there were inexpressible words he heard and things so beyond this earth they would be hard to comprehend. As a result of what Paul saw and heard, he lived his life with a desire for that place after this one. This is why certain scriptures reveal his passion for the heavenly realm. Philippians 1:21-26 shows this struggle that Paul found himself in.

> For to me, to live is Christ, and to die is gain. But if I live on in the flesh, this will mean fruit from my labor; yet what I shall choose I cannot tell. For I am hard-pressed between the two, having a desire to depart and be with Christ, which is far better. Nevertheless to remain in the flesh is more needful for you. And being confident of this, I know that I shall remain and continue with you all for your progress and joy of faith, that your rejoicing for me may be more abundant in Jesus Christ by my coming to you again.

The desire to depart and be with Christ had come from his previous encounter. Perhaps when he was stoned, he died and went into that realm for a time. This left him with a longing in his heart that earth could never fill. Yet his sense of love and responsibility to the church here in the earth caused him to stay. This shows us, somewhat, what an encounter with the heavenly realm can produce.

We see this same passion in Paul in Second Corinthians 5:1-8. Paul calls it a *groaning* that was so intense that he could never be completely fulfilled here. He wanted the heavenly dimension he had encountered.

> *For we know that if our earthly house, this tent, is destroyed, we have a building from God, a house not made with hands, eternal in the heavens. For in this we groan, earnestly desiring to be clothed with our habitation which is from heaven, if indeed, having been clothed, we shall not be found naked. For we who are in this tent groan, being burdened, not because we want to be unclothed, but further clothed, that mortality may be swallowed up by life. Now He who has prepared us for this very thing is God, who also has given us the Spirit as a guarantee.*
>
> *So we are always confident, knowing that while we are at home in the body we are absent from the Lord. For we walk by faith, not by sight. We are confident, yes, well pleased rather to be absent from the body and to be present with the Lord.*

His desire to be absent from the body and present with the Lord could definitely have come from his visit to heaven after he was killed by stoning. However, he was resurrected back to life. Most of us will never make a trip to heaven and then come back. I don't believe this is necessary. We can so experience the resurrection life of

Jesus now that it births in us this passion for the heavenly realm. The truth is that most of the church is carnal today. They are content to just go to heaven when they die. When we have experienced His resurrection life, it should propel us into a new level of desire for Him. Again, Colossians 3:1-3 declares that if we have partaken of His resurrection life, it should create a passion for heavenly things.

> *If then you were raised with Christ, seek those things which are above, where Christ is, sitting at the right hand of God. Set your mind on things above, not on things on the earth. For you died, and your life is hidden with Christ in God.*

Notice that *if we are raised with Christ*, we ought to have a new set of desires that take hold of us. My prayer for all of us is that from our resurrected place we would set our minds on things above. They would captivate us and control us rather than the things of the world. We would be willing to pay a price to have all that we are called to walk in. This is when revival will come and will be a sign that revival has arrived to the church. I am told during the Welsh Revival that bars closed, soccer/football games were suspended, and other worldly activities shut down. This was not because some of them were evil. It was because a revival of His resurrection life had touched the earth. When we are touched by this power, the other things of the world will lose their appeal. The glimmer and shine of fleshly activities will no longer attract us. We have been touched by something greater and more glorious.

> Lord, as I stand in Your Courts, I pray that I would have a passion to encounter the heavenly realm. Forgive me for my carnal desires that outweigh spiritual longing. Let Your resurrection life in me put my mind and attention on heavenly things. May I separate myself to You and what is of You. May the same passion that was in the apostle Paul be in me as well. May my devotion be to You because I have caught a glimpse of Your glory. Therefore, nothing in this world can ever completely satisfy again. Allow me to become a true spiritual person who longs more for the realms of heaven than I do for this earth. Allow this, Lord, to grant me even encounters in Your Courts, where things are rendered because of my status before You. I ask this in Jesus' Name, amen.

What led up to the stoning of Paul, then his resurrection, was the move of the miraculous. The man who had been born crippled was suddenly and miraculously healed. The same resurrection power that raised Paul up was the power he carried to perform the miracle. Ephesians

1:19-20 tells us that the resurrection of Jesus was the greatest demonstration of God's power. This same power is now toward us.

And what is the exceeding greatness of His power toward us who believe, according to the working of His mighty power which He worked in Christ when He raised Him from the dead and seated Him at His right hand in the heavenly places.

Paul was actually praying that our spiritual eyes and awareness would be opened that we might recognize this power. This same power that brought Jesus out of the tomb is now accessible to us. This means nothing is impossible to us. The key to this power is the enlightenment of our eyes. If we can perceive by revelation the power of God toward us, we can access it. Knowing something by revelation is so often the critical key to operating in it. For instance, God told Abraham that however far he could see, that land would be his. We find this in Genesis 13:14-15 when Lot separated from Abraham. The land that Abraham would have was connected to how far he could see.

And the Lord said to Abram, after Lot had separated from him: "Lift your eyes now and look from the place where you are—northward, southward, eastward, and westward; for all the land which you see I give to you and your descendants forever."

Notice that the land that Abraham could see was given to him and his descendants. Could it be that our ability to see also determines what the generations after us get? This means we need to see in faith. People of revelation see what others miss. The result of them seeing something others are not seeing usually leads some to call them fools. However, their ability to see something as possible causes them to introduce things that change the world.

I love to watch shows on the History Channel that are about the machines that made America. There are also ones about the food that made America and other things as well. The constant in all these shows is that there was a person or a handful of people who could see what others couldn't. Whether it was a tractor replacing mules in the field or the invention of cans to preserve food on the shelf for long periods of time, someone imagined it before it was. This is what *seeing* is. It is the power to imagine something and believe in it so strongly that you will not stop until it happens.

Abraham saw what was to be his and his descendants' land. God promised he would give this land to them. There would be a need to possess it, but it was allotted to them by God. What has God promised you? What can you see that others do not? How we see is very important. Remember that God commended Jeremiah on how he saw in Jeremiah 1:11-12. Jeremiah saw a branch of an almond tree. This seemed to actually excite the Lord.

> *Moreover the word of the Lord came to me, saying,
> "Jeremiah, what do you see?"*
>
> *And I said, "I see a branch of an almond tree."*
>
> *Then the Lord said to me, "You have seen well, for I
> am ready to perform My word."*

At this particular stage, Israel as a nation was in decline and backslidden from the Lord. The almond tree is one of the few trees that bud and blossom in the winter. When Jeremiah could see Israel as that almond tree, blossoming and blooming even when in a winter time of being away from God, this did indeed excite God. He knew He had a prophet He could work through. He could *see* in faith and not just the natural circumstances.

As a seeing people, we must not see what is. We must see what can and will be. This allows us to possess the future rather than repeat the past and present. The ability to see is because we have a conviction of the resurrection power of God. That no matter what things might be now, through the resurrection life of Jesus they can and will live again. Paul brought resurrection life to the man who was crippled in his feet. That same resurrection life raised him from the dead when he was stoned. We must be able to see this power that is toward us. When we do, nothing will be impossible to us!

Lord, I pray that You might grant me eyes that are enlightened and can see. May I see the power of God that was demonstrated in Jesus' resurrection and know it is toward me. I ask that any agreement with unbelief that hinders me from seeing as I ought would be revoked. Anything in my bloodline that is empowering this spirit of reason that annihilates faith, would You forgive me for it. Let its rights be revoked and allow me to believe You and see the miraculous of God manifest in the situations of my life. Even as Paul moved in resurrection power and caused the crippled man to be healed, let everything crippled in me be raised to life in Jesus' Name, amen.

CHAPTER 15

SAINTS' RESURRECTION

In examining the different resurrections in the Bible that we might believe for His resurrection power, we mustn't forget the resurrection of the saints after Jesus was raised. They are the firstfruits of the resurrection of the dead that we shall all experience. Matthew 27:50-53 shares with us an amazing occurrence connected to Jesus' resurrection.

> And Jesus cried out again with a loud voice, and yielded up His spirit.
>
> Then, behold, the veil of the temple was torn in two from top to bottom; and the earth quaked, and the rocks were split, and the graves were opened; and many bodies of the saints who had fallen asleep were raised; and coming out of the graves after His resurrection, they went into the holy city and appeared to many.

After the resurrection of Jesus, who had to be the firstfruits from the dead, saints of old were raised and seen. The legal action of Jesus on the cross on our behalf did two things mentioned here. First, the veil in the temple was rent in two from top to bottom. This veil had been set in place by God in the original tabernacle. It allowed God to dwell in the midst of His people, yet kept God and people separated, lest His holiness should bring judgment. Only one man, the high priest, once a year could go behind this veil and commune with God, mostly doing legal work on behalf of the people of God. His work behind that veil would give God the legal right to bless the people rather than judge them for their sin. He would sprinkle the blood of the Passover Lamb in this holiest of holies. This blood would *speak* on behalf of the nation of Israel and roll their sins back for a year. This had to be done every year on the Day of Atonement. Otherwise, the judgments of a holy God would fall on the people of God and the nation of Israel. Hebrews 9:3-8 speaks to us of this veil and what was behind it. It also tells us what the veil did and why it had to be removed.

And behind the second veil, the part of the tabernacle which is called the Holiest of All, which had the golden censer and the ark of the covenant overlaid on all sides with gold, in which were the golden pot that had the manna, Aaron's rod that budded, and the tablets of the covenant; and above it were the cherubim of glory overshadowing the mercy seat. Of these things we cannot now speak in detail.

Now when these things had been thus prepared, the priests always went into the first part of the tabernacle, performing the services. But into the second part the high priest went alone once a year, not without blood, which he offered for himself and for the people's sins committed in ignorance; the Holy Spirit indicating this, that the way into the Holiest of All was not yet made manifest while the first tabernacle was still standing.

The veil being in place was an indication that the way into the Holy of Holies or the Holiest of All was not available to us. Notice that behind this veil was a golden censer and the ark of the covenant. The golden censer speaks of the incense of worship and prayer, while the ark of the covenant speaks to us of the manifest presence of the Lord. With this *presence* was the golden pot of manna that is the *provision of God*. There was also the rod of Aaron that budded. It is the *authority of God*. Then there were the tablets of the covenant that God gave Moses, or the ten commandments. This speaks of the *law or standard of God*.

These three things tell us some of what is contained in the presence and glory of God as we enter it. We can and will experience the provision of the Lord in our life. This is spiritually, within our soul, physically, financially, and every way. God is our provider, and when we enter the Holiest of Holies these things are found in His awesome, glorious presence. Also within this presence is the authority of God. When we move and operate in and from the presence of the Lord, mountains move. We can speak a word and see things come to divine order. Healings occur and many other things, because from the presence of the Lord flows the authority of God.

The other thing mentioned is the word or standard of the Lord. There is also conviction and a pressing of God's standard of holiness and purity that comes from the presence of the Lord. When we come into His presence we become aware of our shortcomings. This is not in a condemning way, but God moves us into His holiness, which is our delight. This is because we are a new creation in Christ Jesus and our old man is dead.

Notice that the veil was ripped from the top to the bottom. On the basis of Jesus' legal work, which His death provided, God could rip away what had separated Him from us and us from Him. No longer would it be one man, one time a year coming into this presence. Now, because of the blood and body of Jesus legally speaking for us, we can enter any time. This is what we are told in Hebrews 10:19-22.

Therefore, brethren, having boldness to enter the Holiest by the blood of Jesus, by a new and living way which He consecrated for us, through the veil, that is, His flesh, and having a High Priest over the house of God, let us draw near with a true heart in full assurance of faith, having our hearts sprinkled from an evil conscience and our bodies washed with pure water.

We now enter the Holiest of All by a new and living way. This is the body and blood of Jesus that was offered. The way has now been made for us enter. We are told to simply come with a true heart, with full assurance of faith, allowing the blood of Jesus to cleanse anything condemning us, and have our body cleansed with water, which I believe is water baptism. We have full access into His glory because when Jesus died on the cross the legal work necessary was done for us! We simply need to put confidence in what Jesus did and know that God has rent the veil separating us because and on the basis of that work!

Lord, as I come before Your Courts, I thank You for all that You have done for me by Your sacrifice. Thank You that when You died on the cross, every legal thing was accomplished. I am now able to enter the holiest of holies because, Lord, You have rent and torn what separated us in two. I take full advantage of this legal rendering and move by faith into Your glorious presence. Thank You that in this presence is provision, authority, and power to live a holy life. Thank You, Lord Jesus, for all that You did legally for me on the cross. Thank You also, Holy Spirit, for helping me as my legal aid to see it fully applied and experienced. I love You and thank You for this in Jesus' Name, amen.

The second thing that happened when Jesus died as He hung on the cross was the graves were *opened*. This means that death and the grave no longer have a power over us. No longer do we die and stay dead. We are brought out of this place because Jesus legally broke the power of death, hell, and the grave. First Corinthians 15:53-57 makes great and astounding statements about our future.

> *For this corruptible must put on incorruption, and this mortal must put on immortality. So when this corruptible has put on incorruption, and this mortal has put on immortality, then shall be brought to pass the saying that is written: "Death is swallowed up in victory."*
>
> *"O Death, where is your sting?*
>
> *O Hades, where is your victory?"*
>
> *The sting of death is sin, and the strength of sin is the law. But thanks be to God, who gives us the victory through our Lord Jesus Christ.*

When Jesus died on the cross, He legally paid the price for anything that would claim the right to hold us in the grave. We are destined to be raised into our own incorruption so we will never die again. Until this time when Jesus died, the righteous who had died were in a *holding place* called Paradise or Abraham's Bosom. They were not permitted to go into the eternal rewards of heaven. This is because there was not a sufficient sacrifice to allow it. The blood of bulls and goats could not cleanse us and do the legal work necessary to see this happen. However, when Jesus died all that was legally required was provided. The moment He died, the graves, or that which held them out of the heaven of God, were opened. Legal payment had been made! This is why we are told "He led captivity captive." This is found in Ephesians 4:8.

> *Therefore He says: "When He ascended on high, He led captivity captive, And gave gifts to men."*

This is a reference to those who had been held in Abraham's Bosom or Paradise. These were waiting for a sufficient sacrifice to legally set things in place that they might go to their eternal rewards. Jesus' death provided this. Notice that even though the graves were opened, they did not come out of the graves until after Jesus' own resurrection. This is because He had to be the firstfruits from the dead. First Corinthians 15:20 declares this is how we know we shall all be raised. He is the firstfruits of those who have slept.

> *But now Christ is risen from the dead, and has become the firstfruits of those who have fallen asleep.*

When the saints came out of the grave after His resurrection, it was a testimony of the consequences of what Jesus had accomplished. Even though their grave and everything legal that was holding them in this place spiritually was now set in place, Jesus had to be the first from the grave. When He arose and took His own blood into the literal Courts of Heaven to speak for us, He carried with him all these that had waited for this to be done. They were now free to move into the next phase of their spiritual existence. The graves that held them were opened, and with Jesus they ascended into heaven and all its glory. Any and every legal claim against us that would cause our grave to be shut was now dealt with by Jesus. His blood and body are now speaking for us and we can no longer be held captive by death. Hebrews 2:14-15 speaks to us of this phenomenon.

> Inasmuch then as the children have partaken of flesh and blood, He Himself likewise shared in the same, that through death He might destroy him who had the power of death, that is, the devil, and release those who through fear of death were all their lifetime subject to bondage.

Jesus death destroyed the legal claims of the devil to torment us with the fear of death. Jesus' death legally destroyed the devil. This releases us from the fear of death and the bondage it places on people. Through Jesus' death, burial, and resurrection, death is no longer a threat. The graves are open, and we will transition into eternal life at our death and receive glorified bodies in the resurrection. All because of Jesus' legal work on our behalf on the cross.

> Lord, as we come before Your Courts, thank You for all that Your death accomplished. Thank You that the grave that was closed and foreboding has now been opened. Lord, You have died and been resurrected. You have ascended on high and led captivity captive. The grave is open and You, Lord, have prevailed. Every threat of the devil is broken. Thank You that I no longer must live with fear of dying. I am free because of all You have done, Lord. Every legal thing that was necessary to my eternal future, Lord, You have provided. I receive this assurance and confidence into my spirit. Thank You so much for this, in Jesus' Name, amen.

CHAPTER 16

LAST DAY
RESURRECTION

As a result of all that Jesus has legally done for us through His sacrifice, we know there will be a resurrection for all saints. We are told and assured that those who belong to Jesus will be raised from the grave with new bodies that transition into the next age. Even though any who presently die are with the Lord at their death, there will be the rejoining with their glorified bodies from the grave. First of all, as we have seen in Second Corinthians 5:8, when we leave our bodies we go into the presence of the Lord.

> *We are confident, yes, well pleased rather to be absent*
> *from the body and to be present with the Lord.*

The moment we die and leave these natural bodies, we are transported into the presence of the Lord Himself. For all who know Him and are in union with Him, this is true. However, our natural bodies are left in the grave.

This is the glory of the last day resurrection. There will be a reunion of our spirit, soul, and body in that day. First Thessalonians 4:13-18 tells us of this wonderful day. When we realize that Jesus has provided everything legally that we need for this to occur, what hope and confidence it brings.

> But I do not want you to be ignorant, brethren, concerning those who have fallen asleep, lest you sorrow as others who have no hope. For if we believe that Jesus died and rose again, even so God will bring with Him those who sleep in Jesus.
>
> For this we say to you by the word of the Lord, that we who are alive and remain until the coming of the Lord will by no means precede those who are asleep. For the Lord Himself will descend from heaven with a shout, with the voice of an archangel, and with the trumpet of God. And the dead in Christ will rise first. Then we who are alive and remain shall be caught up together with them in the clouds to meet the Lord in the air. And thus we shall always be with the Lord. Therefore comfort one another with these words.

Notice that Jesus is going to bring with Him, at His return to earth, those who have already died. Their dead bodies will come out of the graves and be renewed and made supernatural for the next age. They will be reunited with their spirits and souls. Any of us who are yet alive will be caught up with them. There will be this wonderful reunion of those who have already died with those who are yet alive. Philippians 3:20-21 shows us that the body we presently have will be made glorious at this resurrection and reunion.

> *For our citizenship is in heaven, from which we also eagerly wait for the Savior, the Lord Jesus Christ, who will transform our lowly body that it may be conformed to His glorious body, according to the working by which He is able even to subdue all things to Himself.*

By the power of who He is and all that He has done, we will be resurrected into this newness of life, where every aspect of us will be changed. Our spirit, soul, and body will become glorious as He is. Our resurrected bodies will be like Jesus after His resurrection. He was able to walk through walls and appear and disappear before others. We will need these new bodies because flesh and blood cannot inherit the next age. First Corinthians 15:50-58 tells us of this awesome, glorious day.

> *Now this I say, brethren, that flesh and blood cannot inherit the kingdom of God; nor does corruption inherit incorruption. Behold, I tell you a mystery: We shall not all sleep, but we shall all be changed— in a moment, in the twinkling of an eye, at the last*

trumpet. For the trumpet will sound, and the dead will be raised incorruptible, and we shall be changed. For this corruptible must put on incorruption, and this mortal must put on immortality. So when this corruptible has put on incorruption, and this mortal has put on immortality, then shall be brought to pass the saying that is written: "Death is swallowed up in victory."

"O Death, where is your sting?

O Hades, where is your victory?"

The sting of death is sin, and the strength of sin is the law. But thanks be to God, who gives us the victory through our Lord Jesus Christ.

Therefore, my beloved brethren, be steadfast, immovable, always abounding in the work of the Lord, knowing that your labor is not in vain in the Lord.

In the next age, we will need bodies that can live in the earth's atmosphere as well as the heavenly one. This is the kind of body that Jesus has. He still has the marks of His humanity and suffering. We know this because He showed them to Thomas. Yet He is able to transition between heaven and earth. This is the glory of the new body that we will have. This is why we are told that flesh and blood, or these natural bodies in their present state, cannot inherit the kingdom of God. The new bodies we will receive at the resurrection will allow us to live in the earthly realm but also the heavenly one. What an awesome truth. This is all a result of the legal work of Jesus that has redeemed all things to Himself. Death shall no longer have authority and power over anything. It will be swallowed up by life.

> Lord, I thank You for all that You legally did on the cross to redeem me completely to Yourself. Thank You that I am redeemed in my spirit, my soul, and my body. Your work is complete and perfect. Even my body shall be redeemed at the resurrection of the last day. Even now, I receive of this resurrection power into my body should I need healing. My ultimate healing, however, shall be on that day when the reuniting of all Your creation is complete. Thank You so very much. Let it be recorded before Your Courts that I believe, trust, and long for that day. In Jesus' Name, amen.

We need to understand how powerful Jesus' work in His sacrifice was and is. Not only will we be redeemed, even creation itself will be completely redeemed. There will be a new heaven and a new earth. Romans 8:18-23 lets us know that the earth and all creation will be set free from the bondage thrust on it at Adam's fall. At the resurrection of the dead bondage comes off and the new heaven and earth are set in place.

For I consider that the sufferings of this present time are not worthy to be compared with the glory which shall be revealed in us. For the earnest expectation of the creation eagerly waits for the revealing of the sons of God. For the creation was subjected to futility, not willingly, but because of Him who subjected it in hope; because the creation itself also will be delivered from the bondage of corruption into the glorious liberty of the children of God. For we know that the whole creation groans and labors with birth pangs together until now. Not only that, but we also who have the firstfruits of the Spirit, even we ourselves groan within ourselves, eagerly waiting for the adoption, the redemption of our body.

The *revealing of the sons of God* is a reference to the saints' resurrection. When the dead in Christ rise again and we who remain are changed in our bodies, the whole of creation is set free. At this moment in time, all of God's creation will be fully and completely redeemed. Notice this is connected to the resurrection of the saints as the revealed sons of God. Up until this time the earth is groaning and laboring in birth pains. Notice, however, that we too as the sons of God are groaning. We have spoken of this before. Our groaning mixed with the groaning of earth and creation gives birth to the coming of the Lord. His return triggers the resurrection of the dead and the freeing of the earth from its condition. Everything is brought into newness. This is a result of the legal work of Jesus on the cross. His work for us and His creation was so complete that not only will we be redeemed spirit, soul, and body, the earth will too. Second Peter 3:11-13 gives us the promise of the new heaven and new earth. The old earth will vanish away in a fervency of heat. The new heaven and earth will be fashioned.

> *Therefore, since all these things will be dissolved, what manner of persons ought you to be in holy conduct and godliness, looking for and hastening the coming of the day of God, because of which the heavens will be dissolved, being on fire, and the elements will melt with fervent heat? Nevertheless we, according to His promise, look for new heavens and a new earth in which righteousness dwells.*

We are challenged to be a holy people in light of what is being promised. This verse says we *hasten* the coming of the day of God. In other words, through our holy lifestyle and groaning of intercession we speed up the events of history. When the resurrection occurs, the new heaven and new earth are set in place. This is what the apostle John saw in Revelation 21:1. This new heaven and earth are the result of the creation being freed from its bondage.

> *Now I saw a new heaven and a new earth, for the first heaven and the first earth had passed away. Also there was no more sea.*

From my perspective, when we piece together the difference scriptures, we see that the *rapture theology* that has been believed with great prevalence is called into question. If at the resurrection of the saints the earth and creation is freed from its bondage, this would only allow for *one coming of the Lord.* There couldn't be a secret rapture where the dead are resurrected and the saints are whisked away. It would mean there is one coming of the Lord, when all eyes will see Him. The saints who have died are reunited with their now glorified bodies. Those yet alive on the earth are caught up in the air. First Thessalonians 4:15-18 gives insight.

> *For this we say to you by the word of the Lord, that we who are alive and remain until the coming of the Lord will by no means precede those who are asleep. For the Lord Himself will descend from heaven with a shout, with the voice of an archangel, and with the trumpet of God. And the dead in Christ will rise first. Then we who are alive and remain shall be caught up together with them in the clouds to meet the Lord in the air. And thus we shall always be with the Lord. Therefore comfort one another with these words.*

Paul says that by prophetic revelation through the word of the Lord he understood these happenings. The Lord will descend with a shout. The dead in Christ shall rise first. Those who remain shall also then be caught up in the air above the earth. We know from previous scripture that this releases the earth from its bondage. As we are caught up in the air to meet the Lord, under our feet the earth will be transformed in its newness as well as the heavens. We will then come back to the earth and rule and reign with Him forever. The earth is the rulership of man. God gave it to him. The resurrection of the dead in the last day of this age will propel us into this next age. We will forever be with the Lord as we rule and reign with Him always.

May we be comforted with these words and always have hope and joy because of our God who raises dead things back to life. The legal work of Jesus through His death, burial, resurrection, and ascension allows this to be fully seen. We have been executing into place the legal work of Jesus. What I have described is the fullness of this execution of His verdict from the cross. All creation will be redeemed because of Jesus' legal activity and the resurrection power of who He is.

> Lord, as I stand before Your Courts, thank You for all You have legally done through Your suffering and sacrifice. Not only is Your legal work sufficient to redeem me, but also Your entire creation. May I be holy in all my conduct and even groan in travail to see that day of resurrection and redemption fully released. May You descend from the heavens

to reclaim all that is Yours. May the shout and the trumpet bring the dead from the grave. Lord, may those yet alive ascend and be caught up and transformed into the image of Your glorious body. I thank You for this. I thank You that Your legal work of atonement makes this sure. There will be a resurrection of life that triggers all these things. Thank You, wonderful Lord, in Jesus' Name, amen.

ABOUT ROBERT HENDERSON

Robert Henderson is a global apostolic leader who operates in revelation and impartation. His teaching empowers the body of Christ to see the hidden truths of Scripture clearly and apply them for breakthrough results. Driven by a mandate to disciple nations through writing and speaking, Robert travels extensively around the globe, teaching on the apostolic, the Kingdom of God, the "Seven Mountains," and most notably the Courts of Heaven. He has been married to Mary for 42 years. They have six children and five grandchildren. Together they are enjoying life in beautiful Waco, Texas.

INCREASE THE EFFECTIVENESS OF YOUR PRAYERS.

Learn how to release your destiny from Heaven's Courts!

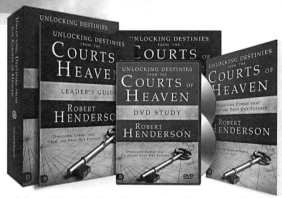

Unlocking Destinies from the Courts of Heaven

Curriculum Box Set Includes:
9 Video Teaching Sessions (2 DVD Disks), Unlocking Destinies *book,*
Interactive Manual, Leader's Guide

There are books in Heaven that record your destiny and purpose. Their pages describe the very reason you were placed on the Earth.

And yet, there is a war against your destiny being fulfilled. Your archenemy, the devil, knows that as you occupy your divine assignment, by default, the powers of darkness are demolished. Heaven comes to Earth as God's people fulfill their Kingdom callings!

In the *Unlocking Destinies from the Courts of Heaven* book and curriculum, Robert Henderson takes you step by step through a prophetic prayer strategy. By watching the powerful video sessions and going through the Courts of Heaven process using the interactive manual, you will learn how to dissolve the delays and hindrances to your destiny being fulfilled.